IGNITE YOUR DORMANT SUPERPOWERS

IGNITE YOUR DORMANT SUPERPOWERS

STEVE DICKASON

CAFFEINE FOR THE BRAIN PUBLICATIONS

© 2018 by Steven Dickason
All rights reserved. No part of this publication may be reproduced, distributed, or transmitted in any form or by any means, including photocopying, recording, or other electronic or mechanical methods, without the prior written permission of the publisher, except in the case of brief quotations embodied in critical reviews and certain other noncommercial uses permitted by copyright law.
For permission requests, write to the publisher at the address below.

Publisher: CaffeineForTheBrain.com

ISBN: 978-1-7323269-6-5

Edited by Jan Johnson, Drantell Publishing and Editing—
Editing by Bob Cooper
Cover & book design by Jim Shubin, BookAlchemist.net

I dedicate this book to the many mentors who taught me that my life path is decided by the choices I make. In addition to the inspirational authors I've studied with, read and listened to through the years, I want to thank the members of JOLT, my weekly discussion group who went on this journey of discovery with me—with special thanks to Gina, my life partner, whose insights, love, support and editing skills were instrumental in the completion of this project.

Thanks to my children, Moorea and Brittany who taught me the meaning of unconditional love, Tarik Ragab for his inspirational creativity, and to all those contentious rascals who challenged me to grow and learn. Couldn't have done this without you.

Finally, I am grateful for the great team of professionals I met through Book Passage—Pathway to Publishing: Jan Johnson Drantell for helping to shape and organize my thoughts; Bob Cooper for his painstaking line-by-line editing; and Jim Shubin, Book Alchemist, for transforming a Word document into a beautiful cover and interior.

CONTENTS

- 9 INTRODUCTION
- 13 CHAPTER 1: The Power to Change Your World— by Changing Yourself
- 39 CHAPTER 2: The Power of Personal Responsibility
- 55 CHAPTER 3: The Power of Using Your Fear to Change Your Life
- 66 CHAPTER 4: The Power to Control Judgment
- 84 CHAPTER 5: Powerfully Bad Words
- 96 CHAPTER 6: The Power of Acceptance— Resistance is Futile
- 107 CHAPTER 7: The Power of Unconditional Happiness
- 116 CHAPTER 8: The Power of Thanksgiving— NOT JUST AN EXCUSE FOR THINNING OUT THE TURKEY POPULATION
- 131 CHAPTER 9: The Power of Creativity
- 141 CHAPTER 10: The Power of Super Listening
- 156 CHAPTER 11: The Power to Remain Calm in the Eye of the Storm
- 168 CHAPTER 12: The Power to Attract Your Teachers
- 174 SUGGESTED READING

INTRODUCTION

Take a moment to gaze at your image in a full-length mirror. The person you see has everything they need to be happy, fulfilled, loved and crazy prosperous. If this has not been your experience to date, take heart. All you need to live the life of your dreams is to locate and liberate amazing powers you currently possess—your innate SuperPowers!

I love superheroes.

My personal favorite has always been Superman because… well, he can fly. As a young boy, during the warm summers in Boulder, Colorado, I spent blissful hours lying on my back in the cool grass at the side of my parents' house, imagining myself soaring through the sky. Smashing through clouds, racing to the sun and back, it was…it was…freedom, pure and simple. No limits. No doubts.

My favorite season was always spring when warm Chinook winds tore through Boulder Canyon with gusts clocked as high as 150 mph. Chinook means snow-eater in the native tongue because a day of Chinooks can melt a foot of snow off the ground. Native Americans are known to have left Boulder in the spring because of the wind. But for me, the Chinooks were like Christmas, Thanksgiving, and the last day of any school year—take your pick—all wrapped up into one.

These mythic winds only last for a few days each year, so my buddies and I would spend every possible moment running down the sidewalk into the blinding wind, holding the sides of our coats out as far as we could—hoping to, of course, fly. Here's where my story gets a little weird. For years after graduating from C.U., I had this wonderful recurring dream:

The Chinooks are howling—must be more than 100 mph—I'm alone, running down a steep hill, holding tight to the sides of my jacket. I lean forward, somehow knowing, trusting, that I will not summersault down the rocky slope and break every bone in my body. The wind pounds the inside of my dark brown corduroy jacket, but I hold tight, let go of the ground and…fly! I'm only a few feet off the ground, but I am flying down the hill.

Did I do it—pull a Wright Brothers sans Kitty Hawk on a hill behind my parents' home?

For many years, I believed that this clandestine flight did happen, that I fearlessly laid out into that roaring Chinook and soared down the hill. I also secretly mused that this might be, could be a sign, that maybe I did have latent SuperPowers, that maybe I was destined to become the second coming of Superman but had not yet, you know, come into my powers. I don't think I ever expressed that feeling to anyone at the time, especially not to Elaine, my first wife. Our young marriage, which began deteriorating during the honeymoon in Disneyland, had enough problems without her thinking I was a whacked-out superhero wannabe.

As the years passed, the dreams came less and less frequently and eventually abandoned my sleeping hours altogether. I'm not sure exactly when I lost my belief in flying and subsequent superhero career, but probably after:

1. My sad and nasty divorce from Elaine.
2. The realization that the best job a marketing degree would produce was management trainee at an F.W. Woolworth store.
3. Sometime after I quit Woolworth's to become a writer, when I didn't sell a single short story after a year, ran out of money and became a delivery truck driver.

Introduction

4. Could have been after I quit driving the truck and started a small business designing, building and *not* selling planter-lights—not selling because purchasers could add a plant (duh). After a year of sending them samples for testing, Underwriters Laboratories informed me that, since they couldn't regulate the final weight, a heavy plant plus fixture might fall and puncture a hole in someone's waterbed. Soooo Seventies.
5. Might have even been after I folded the planter-light business to write and sell songs, which apparently only my mother and I loved. (I had been in a rock band from ninth grade through college.)

Somewhere along the way, I let these events and others end any hope I had of becoming a superhero. I decided to settle for a "normal," unspectacular life. No saving people in distress, no fighting evil and, of course, no flying. From a less DC Comics perspective, I was ready to settle for less than I once thought I might accomplish. Forget my dream of making a living through some creative endeavor. I would never hear my songs on the radio, would not see my stories in magazines or my books in any library. I would work, make enough money to get by, maybe get married again and have 2.5 children—the ideal number according to Gallup, although I would probably round that number up or down. And then, you know, die.

My story is, of course, not unique. Having taught and counseled hundreds of salespeople, nearly every one of them had a similar story. So, what happens? What kind of butt-kicking does it take to transform confident, limitless children into fearful, unhappy, over-medicated adults? Why do our parents, teachers, friends, enemies, even complete strangers conspire to burst our bubble, kill off our dreams, strip us of our powers? The answer may surprise you.

Liberating your SuperPowers will give you the tools you need to live a self-directed life—the life of your dreams; not the life others want for you and not the small life for which you may think you have to settle. Getting excited? Having guided many would-be superheroes through this process, I'm excited to be guiding you.

The life you've always wanted to live is within your grasp. The Powers you need to achieve this life you already have. Liberate your hidden powers, and you'll be flying in no time. Let's get started.

CHAPTER 1

THE POWER TO CHANGE YOUR WORLD BY CHANGING YOURSELF!

SUPERPOWER:
The willingness, commitment, passion and courage to change your world by changing yourself.

Self-Examination: Are you willing to look within and ask yourself whether you are doomed to lead an ordinary, mediocre life, or meant for something better, something special? Do you want to change? Are you willing to change? If yes, when? These are questions you'll need to answer before going on to Chapter 2.

It takes energy and passionate intention to ignite your inner SuperPowers. You must want it bad. So bad that your desire rises to the level of knowing—knowing that the life of your dreams is yours, just around the corner, rushing at you as sure as your next gas and electric bill, but a lot more fun.

I've been to a few AA and Al-Anon meetings. They are wonderful organizations where attendees describe "hitting bottom" as a primary catalyst for their recovery. The basic idea is that, for things to get better, they must first get worse. Only then can they admit they have a problem and seek help.

We need not fall to rise, but it does seem to strengthen the resolve to change. Whether you've hit bottom or not, you must at least get pissed off enough with your current state that you will do almost anything to change.

Hitting bottom doesn't have to come in the form of your fourth DUI or your spouse walking out on you with the UPS delivery person. Your bottom might be when you realize that your favorite chair is the one you constructed out of old pizza boxes and duct tape, or perhaps when you notice that you have dedicated an entire drawer in your kitchen to little packs of parmesan and red peppers. It doesn't matter what your bottom looks like (unless you're into yoga) if it creates the reaction we saw in the 1976 Oscar-winning film, *Network*:

> "I want you to get MAD! I don't want you to protest. I don't want you to riot. I don't want you to write to your congressman, because I wouldn't know what to tell you to write. I don't know what to do about the depression and the inflation and the Russians and the crime in the street. All I know is that first, you've got to get mad. You've got to say: "I'm a human being, goddamn it! My life has value!" So, I want you to get up now. I want all of you to get up out of your chairs. I want you to get up right now and go to the window. Open it, and stick your head out, and yell: "I'M AS MAD AS HELL, AND I'M NOT GOING TO TAKE THIS ANYMORE!"

Ah, go ahead, do it. You know you want to; who cares what the neighbors think. They'd like to do it too. Maybe you'll start a trend in the 'hood. Go to the window!

As I mentioned in the Introduction, I had interpreted a series of setbacks as failures rather than the way I see them now—steppingstones on the path of life. I'd also committed a double sin. In addition to calling them failures, I was quick to lay the blame on anything or anyone but me. At that time, personal responsibility was not part of my vocabulary. This misinterpretation left me feeling dejected, rejected and not in the mood to be inspected. I did not want to be around people for fear of being judged for my apparent long list of shortcomings. I became reclusive, non-communicative—yes, a whiny little punk.

By my mid-twenties I had buried my SuperPowers under such a massive pile of fear and self-doubt that mediocrity was becoming a way of life. I had misplaced the belief that I had powers waiting to burst forth, and replaced it with acceptance of an ordinary, powerless life. But even after deciding I would never fly (again?), there was always a faint flicker of hope. An irritating little voice would pop up right when I was choosing to play it safe, feeling relief, hidden well within my comfort zone. *Really*, it would whisper, *I'm not going to be special? This is my life?* The same challenging message Christopher Pike gave Captain Kirk in J.J. Abrams' *Star Trek*:

"You can settle for a less than ordinary life, or do you feel like you were meant for something better? Something special?"

Breaking out of a habitual, less than fulfilling life can be challenging. The world is overrun with people living average, unhappy lives, just getting by (or not), and mediocrity is like gravity: It attempts to pull down everyone it encounters. Just listen to the banter between check-out clerks and customers at your local grocery store.

Clerk: "How you doing this morning?"

Customer: "You know, DDSS—different day, same shit," or "Fine, but it's still morning, give it time," or simply, "Don't ask."

Clerk: "I hear ya."

It takes focused attention to reject the negative bias so prevalent in society—to choose to create a better life and take the actions that will bring it to fruition.

Another reason why so many choose to settle for an "ordinary life" is that liberating SuperPowers, growing into the person you think you might be and experiencing a better, special life causes your body to leak—you know, sweat. It's work. It requires you to do what most people fear more than just about anything—**change**. Oh no! Not that!

Do you possess the willingness and the power required to change your world? Okay, I'm not talking about flying faster than a speeding bullet, leaping tall buildings in a single bound or melting stuff with x-ray vision. **Your powers are what you need—to be who you choose to be—to achieve the life you want to live.**

I knew that I had once felt special—you know, the second coming of Superman and all that. How far I had fallen. How could my self-esteem have sunk so low? Even Mighty Mouse-like miniaturized powers were beyond my expectations. The journey to regain a healthy self-image and liberate my SuperPowers has been a gratifying, fulfilling and, I've discovered, lifelong process, one that I will discuss in future chapters.

You are now at one of several crossroads you will encounter in this book—as in life. If you are happy with your current life or have yet to hit bottom, I guess it's goodbye. But the fact that you were attracted to and are reading this book is a strong indication that you would like to consider a change. Deciding to not only live but to live life on my terms was the beginning of my process to find and liberate my inner SuperPowers—the indispensable first step, a step you will need to take if you decide to reject the ordinary, if you sense that you were meant for something better. Something special.

So, now it's your turn to decide. Can't you just see Clint Eastwood staring you down with those steely eyes and, of course, his .44 Magnum Smith and Wesson Model 29 revolver:

"You've got to ask yourself one question. Do I feel special? Well, do ya, punk?"

Yeah, I know the line was "Do I feel lucky?" but that doesn't fit the circumstance, and it is my book after all. And since it's an interactive book, it is your turn to speak. I can wait: no problem. Are you willing to settle for your current life or do you want something better, a more fulfilling and rewarding life? I'll even leave some blank space for your response:

There is no judgment here. Each day you are faced with two choices:
1. Re-create the past by thinking the same old thoughts and taking the same old habitual actions, which will result in predictable, comfortable, repetitive experiences; or
2. Grow. Stop defining and thereby limiting yourself. Respond in new, unpredictable ways. Question what you "know." Take risks. Enjoy new experiences and make the most of your precious time on this planet. But, like it or not, growth requires change. Change requires:

   - a new attitude
   - new actions
   - new habits and behaviors

Evolution (change) is no walk in the park. It is often a violent, dangerous process that pushes us far outside our comfort zones. Our self-limiting, protective belief system prefers the safety of the status quo. It restricts our actions to minimize risk, anxiety, stress. Limitations like:

- Trying hard just causes others to resent me. Nobody likes a showoff.
- If I get that promotion, they're going to discover how little I know.
- Making more money means I'll have more to lose.

Choosing the status quo—living a comfortable life with minimal risk and stress—is, of course, a choice, one that most people seem to make. I am not saying that this choice is better or worse than the alternative—making whatever changes are necessary to live the life of your dreams, discovering and exploring your potential. We each have a precious life to live and how we live it is our business, *as long as we do not hurt others*. There are, however, consequences to our choices.

So, what's the problem with just remaining within the safety of your comfort zone? Sounds, you know, comfortable.

Researchers in the Psychology of Human Productivity have found that remaining within the comfort zone, where you experience minimal risk and anxiety, results in *limited, predictable productivity*. In other words, playing it safe is a path to mediocrity. But, even in the face of stacks and stacks of data and experience, most people still find it less frightening to live within their imagined limitations, disappointments and mediocrity than to initiate real change. The thinking goes something like this:

"I may not like my life, but at least I understand it; I'm used to it. I know the rules, and there aren't a lot of surprises." This is the anthem of people we all know who have chosen the status quo—what they believe is a risk-free, stress-free life.

The problem with hiding within your comfort zone is that it does *not* provide the security or peace you crave. There you sit, day in/day out, thinking you "know" how life works, expending enormous amounts of time and energy attempting to manipulate the world so that your beliefs are proven right. This makes you feel safe and secure but ultimately leads to a world without surprises, adventure, learning or growth, and probably no friends, since no one likes hearing that they're wrong all the time. And lots and lots of suffering. Sound like fun yet?

In 1966, Robert F. Kennedy delivered a speech that included this line:

"There is a Chinese curse which says, 'May we live in interesting times.'"

Like it or not, we live in interesting times. It is a time of danger and uncertainty, yes, but also the most creative, innovative time in the history of the world. Many interpret this "curse" to mean that uninteresting times of peace are more life-enhancing. I say bollocks—or I would if I were British.

I don't think this is a curse at all, but a very positive, life-affirming statement. Uninteresting times make us feel comfortable and secure because they match our peaceful, simplistic, grossly inaccurate model of the world. To live in interesting times, times of challenge and difficulty, advances our learning, our growth. It enhances and expands our lives.

Remember what Helen Keller said about security:

"Security is mostly a superstition. It does not exist in nature, nor do the children of men, as a whole, experience it. Avoiding danger is no safer in the long run than outright exposure. Life is either a daring adventure or nothing."

Don't you love this, especially coming from a woman who was born deaf and blind? What courage and appreciation for the rare gift of life.

An antonym for change is *stagnation*. The word just sounds nasty, conjuring up images of mold or slimy green algae in a small mountain lake, or that jerky chick who crawls out of your TV in *The Ring*. No one wants to be seen as a person who would intentionally choose to rot and crawl. Yet every day, people select stagnation over change. After all, change forces us from our comfortable, *known* world into the frightening, dangerous unknown.

Okay, okay, I know I said that I don't judge people who choose a status quo existence, and that's true—for the most part (hey, I'm not perfect, just a work in progress). I do differentiate, however, between those people who accept their choices and those who relentlessly complain about them to the rest of us. Angrily complaining about one's limitations while doggedly defending them is, in my opinion, a cry for help. It says to me:

"This is the choice I made. I don't like it, but there's nothing I can do about it." Or worse:

"Fate dealt me this hand. Nothing I can do about it."

People who read this book will have one of two dramatic reactions: *Victims* who see their plight as a condition imposed by circumstances of birth, location, upbringing, etc., are angered by the implication that they have choices. I know this because of the hate mail I've received from some of my published articles. Ironically, believing that they are powerless allows them to retain a sense of power and self-esteem. But then there are those *self-directed* people who will receive this news like an oasis in the desert, have an epiphany and begin exploring their possibilities—and start searching for their hidden SuperPowers.

Okay, are you thoroughly convinced that change is necessary for growth? If you need a little more convincing, here are the words of some people you may have heard of:

Gandhi said:
"If you choose to change your world, begin with yourself."
"Be the change you wish to see in the world."

And from Neville Goddard (1905-1972), a prophet, profoundly influential teacher and author:

"Good news! If you don't like what you're manifesting, you can change your mind about who you are."

Not yet convinced? Let's try Einstein—scientist, spiritualist and well-known brilliant guy:

"The world as we have created it is a process of our thinking. It cannot be changed without changing our thinking."

Let's add some international flavor since WE ARE A COUNTRY OF IMMIGRANTS! This is from the Persian poet, Rumi:

"Yesterday I was clever, so I wanted to change the world. Today I am wise, so I am changing myself."

Okay, one more, since we are trying to improve relations with Russia, from Tolstoy:

"Everyone thinks of changing the world, but no one thinks of changing himself."

Assuming you're still with me on this journey, let's explore the question of how and what we change. Many have made the mistake of trying to change circumstances rather than changing themselves; this flawed tactic is sometimes called the "geographic cure." Real estate agents are a very mobile sales force: every year a high percentage of agents change brokers. Their business falls off due to the economy, rising interest rates, too many bad hair days, a sudden interest in daytime soaps, early-onset narcolepsy or whatever, so they decide that changing where they work will somehow energize them—"take my career to the next level."

You probably know someone who moves from job to job, career to career, but never seems to experience an increase in their income or sense of accomplishment. The problem with changing where they work, where they live, or what career they pursue is that it prevents them from effecting real, lasting change—change that can only come from within. Thus the saying:

"No Matter Where You Go, There You Are." —

The Adventures of Buckaroo Banzai Across the 8th Dimension

You can't escape yourself by running. You can change your circumstances, your location, your profession, your friends, but wherever you go and whatever you do, there you are. And if you are *not* willing to change, to adapt, to learn, no matter where you go, you will do what it takes to perpetuate the status quo, replicate your old environment, no matter how dysfunctional.

Dr. Richard Carlson, author of *Don't Sweat the Small Stuff,* once had a man who lived on the East Coast ask him, "What are people like in California?" To which Dr. Carlson responded, "What are people like in New York?" The man answered, "They're greedy and selfish." Dr. Carlson told the man that he would probably find the people in California also to be greedy and selfish. Why? Our judgments, beliefs, perceptions and habits do not change just because of a change in location or circumstance—we carry them with us.

My mom was a beautiful person who loved her father very much. When he was eight years old, living in rural Kansas, my grandfather, Benjamin Franklin Henderson, was given the job of walking the rails at night, looking for dangerous breaks in the track. To keep him warm, his mother would send him out with a heavy coat, a hat, gloves and a tin of hot toddy—that's booze. One night, armed with his oil lantern and toddy, little Benjamin stumbled onto a washed-out bridge which would have caused a massive and deadly derailment. He ran for miles until the lights of an oncoming train came into view. Exhausted, little Ben fell to his knees in the middle of the track and flagged the train down with his lantern. When they realized what a disaster he had prevented, the passengers poured out of the train and filled my grandfather's hat with money.

He was a brave little boy, and an alcoholic by the time he

was ten. Benjamin died when my mom was a young girl. My Mom was married five times, each husband an alcoholic. Every time a marriage failed she would inevitably fall in love with another drunk. Changing husbands over and over was apparently not the answer to duplicating the love she felt for her father. Had she understood her subconscious criteria for choosing partners, she could have modified her beliefs about what she deserved and what loving male relationships looked like, and perhaps have found a more nurturing and sober partner.

How do we become agents of change?

Success requires change; so how do you become more comfortable with change? How do you become more comfortable with anything? Repetition. You practice until the unfamiliar becomes familiar. If you have resisted change in the past, here are a few tips. No extra charge.

1. **Form a new habit.** Change is not something to be feared or procrastinated. Begin by making small, intentional changes in your life until they become more natural, comfortable activities. Change the color or style of your hair. Shop at a grocery store you've never patronized. Drive a new route to work. Eat something you swore you'd never eat (not sushi! —but that's just me).

2. **Change your focus.** Emerson said, "You are what you think about all day long." A corollary to Emerson's quote is, "You get what you resist." If you focus on the current, limited aspects of your life, you will continue to behave and act in ways that support your limitations. Key to manifesting change is to become the change you choose to

incorporate into your life. Think and act as if it has already come to pass and you engage the assistance of your subconscious—you sensitize your perception to make you aware of opportunities, and teachers. **See beyond the closed door and it will open as if by magic.**

3. **Get comfortable with fear.** We use fear to prevent change (see Chapter 4). When you are about to have an experience that is outside your comfort zone, you create a fear response to motivate yourself back to your known world. Let's say that you believe you have a fear of heights. When a person you'd love to date asks you to go to an amusement park to ride the roller coasters, you experience fear. If you choose to avoid the stress and anxiety of living outside your feel-good zone, you will find a way *not* to be able to go on the date—haircut appointment, IRS audit… When you become a "change agent," when you understand that fear is a tool you engage to stay within your known world, you can choose to experience the fear, ride the roller coaster, get the date and, yes, probably throw up. Fear, after all, won't kill you—not quickly anyway. Remember Franklin D. Roosevelt's famous words, "There is nothing to fear but fear itself." Alternatively, you could decide to modify your underlying beliefs about heights that are causing you to utilize the fear response. Fortunately, you can edit or delete any viewpoint you currently have—more on that in future chapters.

4. **Be mindful of the objects of your gratitude.** You can communicate your desire for change to your subconscious by what you are grateful for. If you give thanks only when the world meets your expectations, mirrors the world within your comfort zone, you trap yourself in the past. The message to your subconscious is that you only want to experience that which you know and expect, choking off any opportunity for growth, learning and adventure. Give thanks when things do not go the way you want and your subconscious will reward you with new, adventurous experiences. If you make a sales presentation but lose out to a competitor, your immediate reaction may be anger, disgust, or jealousy toward the one who closed the sale. Instead, give thanks that you dared to make the appointment that created the opportunity to practice your presentation. Be grateful that you learned from an experience that helped you sharpen your presentation skills for the future. Be thankful that you met some new people; perhaps your paths will cross again someday. Do that and you will be amazed at how many presentation opportunities come your way.

Change Yourself, Not Your Circumstances

"A higher concept of yourself involves taking on new truths and shedding old views of what is achievable. This is the only way you can achieve your desires." — *Wayne Dyer*

Deciding what you want out of life is essential. But you will only achieve your desires when they are congruent with who you think you are (your self-concept). So, who are you? One way to analyze self is to divide it between the Outer Self concept and the Inner Self concept.

The outer self is what you've constructed within your comfort zone. It consists of what you believe you are capable of and not capable of doing, thinking and feeling, based on personal experience and the opinions of others. It's important to keep in mind that this construct is *not who you are*, just *who you have decided you are*—a decision that can be modified. The process of creating and maintaining your outer self begins at birth (or before) and continues until death.

The inner self is an expanded view of who you are. In 1976, researchers Franks and Marolla wrote that the "sense of inner self derives from feelings of one's efficacy and competence." It is not as affected by concerns over how your actions will be perceived by the outside world. It is your innermost feelings, the values you cherish most.

The gap between the two selves can create a lot of suffering. As a kid, my inner self felt that I would be good at sports, while my outer self believed that I would be ridiculed and embarrassed if I tried out for a team. So, I never did. As a young adult, my inner self knew that I would be a good teacher and public speaker. My outer self cringed at the thought of standing up in front of an audience. But I'm happy to tell you that my outer self lost that battle. Read on.

Changing your self-concept is a process of rejecting or modifying your 'outer' concept so that it is more in line with your 'inner' concept. It could go something like this:

1. **Get to know your inner self.** What are your core values and beliefs?
2. **Decide to change.** Be willing to accept the uncertainty of change, to face the unknown, to lose control (as if you ever had it).
3. **Be willing to relinquish the ordinary life.** To achieve, to become something more, something special, you must give up the comfort of the life you know (or think you do), face your fears and embrace the daring adventure. Reject the limitations you have placed on yourself, often at the suggestion of others.
4. **Lay siege to the fortress.** Altering or eliminating firmly held beliefs, the beliefs that you think bring you security, will naturally create resistance. Your outer self, from its home within the comfort zone, will fight to maintain the status quo it believes necessary for survival. Hang tough. Your comfort zone is yours. You created it. You can alter it. You're the boss!
5. **Changing a very threatened 'outer' image requires patience and persistence,** fueled by a burning desire to become more. You must want change more than you need the security you believe comes from living within your chosen limitations. Tough it out. You'll win in the end.

You Must Be PC – Passionate and Committed

Real change requires commitment and passion. An attendee at one of my goal achievement workshops told me that he was comfortable with his income but, since it was a goals class, he would set a goal to earn 30 percent more the next year—and maybe go on a nice long vacation with the extra money. In a later conversation, it was evident that the reality of what was required to achieve his goal had set in. He would have to make more phone calls and even walk door-to-door prospecting for listings, something he did not believe he could do without considerable discomfort. He was afraid. The perceived stress of increasing his performance exceeded his desire for the reward of higher income. The goal went into a desk drawer.

Time for Human Trials

After years of study, I was ready to transform theory into action. And what better guinea pig than me? For roughly the first half of my life, I was limited and controlled by a rather severe case of social anxiety. All my important life decisions were greatly influenced by a strong desire to avoid human interaction, judgement, criticism. I knew I needed to change—something. One cold fall morning, I left my little house and took a long walk around the neighborhood with the intention of making a momentous decision. I would either decide to depart this life or change it. Simple, really, and so Shakespearian: "To be or not to be," hell of a question. That was my bottom. I was mad as hell and had no intention of taking it anymore!

It was no longer acceptable to be in constant fear of people, their judgments, and ultimate rejection. It *had* to stop, one way or another. And, frankly, at that point, I didn't much care which way it went. I guess, since you're reading this, you can figure out how I decided to proceed.

During that walk, I had an epiphany: If I were to grow into

the amazing person I once thought I could be, I would have to break through my fear of personal interaction. Easy to say now; not so easy back then. I had lived with nearly constant fear and anxiety most of my life. I had tried several things to make myself more acceptable to people—especially female-type people. When I was in the ninth grade, I decided to take steps. I took up weightlifting and gained 30 pounds of muscle; I joined a rock band and became the lead singer. There I was, a muscular rock singer. *Wow*, what more could teenage girls want? Obviously something, because it didn't work. I became haunted by images of being the last virgin at my high school, of having the caption under my senior yearbook picture read: "Most likely to *never* have sex."

Now, here I was at age 26, taking my Shakespearian walk, still experiencing the same fear, the same self-doubt. I decided to try one last thing—something radical. I would pursue the most terrifying career I could ever imagine—selling real estate. The thought of calling strangers, going to their homes, attempting to sell myself and my services, was bone-numbingly terrifying. That very day, with shaky hands and a dirt-dry mouth, I signed up for a California real estate licensing course. That's when I began reading everything I could find on personal growth, achievement, facing fear. You name it, I read it, listened to it on tape or attended workshops about it. After several years of study, it was time for human trials. Getting into real estate sales was a significant step in my war against a horrible self-image. At the time, what I thought I knew about myself was pitiful. I was shy, unattractive, inarticulate, and terrified of being noticed and judged by others. Perfect material for a charismatic, dynamic and successful real estate agent—or not.

Indulge me while I give you a little more background on what life was like before discovering my powers. Your conclusion, from listening to my story, will hopefully be: "If he can do that—transform from a highly functioning recluse with low self-esteem and a fear of human interaction into a confident, comfortable speaker/trainer/coach—I can do as much. I can finally create the life I've always imagined."

I first noticed my anxiety in elementary school. The thought of taking part in any group activity, like dodge ball or kickball, was terrifying. I was sure that if I made a mistake, I would be mocked, humiliated, and probably pantsed and tied to the flagpole—upside down. I would avoid taking part in these activities whenever possible—fake illness, hide in a tree at the far end of the play yard, hijack a plane headed for Cuba, creative stuff like that.

I was in the ninth grade when I discovered how far I would go to avoid being noticed. I was in class with a bladder near the point of bursting. In those days, if you wanted to leave the classroom for the bathroom, you had to raise your hand indicating with one finger that you had to pee or two fingers to poo. There was no way I would suffer the attention and humiliation of raising my hand and revealing my elimination preference. So I concocted a bold and desperate plan.

The class was nearly over, and I only lived a few blocks from the school. Two minutes before the bell; time to execute. I released my bladder and felt the warm liquid expand to cover the front of my jeans. So far, so good—sort of. There was a door in that room that led directly out to the track. The bell rang. I held my books, strategically covering the giant wet patch on my jeans, and walked quickly out the door, across the field and home to change. No one ever knew—no one but me. Great self-esteem builder.

One day I remember setting up for a gig at the Tiki Teen Club, where our band played regularly. Linda, a girl I was very interested in (from afar, of course), was sitting at the soda bar with friends. One of her buddies came over to me and said, "You know, Linda likes you. She told me to tell you that if you ask her out, she will say yes." No brainer, right? How could I possibly blow this opportunity? Easily, as it turned out. Even though there was no reason to disbelieve what her friend was telling me, I was sure that in the end, Linda would reject me. I ignored the offer—hating myself more than ever. I went home that night and thought of Linda—all night long.

A few years later, when I was a senior in high school, our band had a manager. And our manager had a secretary. She was probably five years older than me—a beautiful, confident, sensuous young woman who made me so nervous I could barely speak to her. She used to flirt with me a lot, even hinting that I should ask her out. Of course, I didn't buy it. Had to be a catch. Her frustration reached the point where she finally asked me out to a drive-in movie. I remember the confusing mixture of strong desire and powerful fear—in seemingly equal doses. Since it would have been more embarrassing to say no, with great trepidation, I agreed. I drove. This was before bucket seats. During the film, she kept moving closer and closer to me until I could feel her leg against mine. I nearly had my first orgasm (with a live woman, that is, who was in the same room as me—at the same time). She did everything but crawl onto my lap, and I didn't as much as kiss or even put my arm around her. But she was persistent, if not a bit masochistic. When I drove her home, she asked if I'd like to come in. Can you imagine how much I wanted to follow her into that house? Since the onset of puberty, I had been frustrated by numerous lost opportunities and here was the most obvious, straightforward offer I had ever received. I was minutes away from seeing an actual naked woman, outside of the pages of *Playboy*. I, of course, rejected the invitation, went home and broke into my parents' liquor cabinet. I was miserable—dreamt that night of inventing a time machine so that I could have a second chance (many second chances by then). She was not happy—got her revenge the next week by having car sex with our drummer. Grrrr.

One more to show the depth of my condition: I took an anatomy class in high school and became fascinated with the topic, becoming the top student in all of the anatomy classes at the school. I studied advanced medical journals my dad borrowed from the library at the National Bureau of Standards in Boulder and wrote unusually detailed and complex reports for a high school class. I was excited to start college, where I would study to become a forensic scientist.

During my second year at C.U., I dropped out of the School of Arts and Sciences and moved over to the School of Business. Why give up my dream of a career in medicine? At that time, the university had a policy that every student in Arts and Sciences had to pass two years of a foreign language. Shouldn't have been a big problem. Except that I was terrified at the prospect of speaking in class, repeating phrases out loud and being the object of ridicule. For several weeks, I convinced myself that I couldn't find the classroom, even though I had lived in Boulder from the age of five and knew the campus well. When it became evident that I couldn't possibly pass the course without attending classes, I petitioned to drop French. It was too late in the semester, so I elected to take an 'F,' the only one I ever received. And since they wouldn't waive the foreign language requirement, I sadly abandoned my dream of a career in medicine and spent two boring years at the school of business. Working in real estate sales was a desperate step toward facing my fear of people. But it was not enough. I was doing the work but was fearful most of the time. I needed to do more, needed to dramatically reduce the anxiety so that I could enjoy more of life and be more productive—even prosperous—even happy?

While my inner self had an idea that I could be a good teacher/trainer, my outer self was rolling on the floor in a fit of laughter. "Not a chance," it yelled. "You get the sweats just ordering pizza!" It was true. So, what better way to discover whether what I'd learned about achievement, self-concepts and the comfort zone was genuine and helpful or just a bunch of New Age drivel. I decided to become a public speaker.

I had studied with Shakti Gawain, author of *Creative Visualization*, learning about the power of visualization. There are hundreds of studies in the use of imagery. Dr. Judd Baslotto of the University of Chicago divided college students into three groups. Each group visited the basketball court where they shot free throws, recording the percentage of made baskets. Then for 30 days, each group followed specific instructions. Group three did not practice or visualize free throws at all. Group two went to the gym and practiced shooting one hour each day. Group one merely imagined shooting free throws without even stepping into a gym. The results were astounding. Group three, which did not practice or visualize, showed no improvement. Group two, which practiced daily, improved by 24 percent. Group one, which only imagined shooting, improved by 23 percent. Since then it has been proven over and over that the subconscious does not discriminate between physical experience and that which is regularly and passionately imagined.

So, hey, I thought I'd give it a try. I would use visualization to convince my outer self that I was not a terrified little wimp, that I was an accomplished and compelling public speaker. Massive stretch for me—hard to believe that I could transform myself from a terrified recluse, uncomfortable interacting with even small groups of friends, into a dynamic, energetic, charismatic public speaker. I decided to conduct a test run to see if I could alter long-term behaviors through the imagery exercises I had learned.

Test Run – Road Rage

I considered myself a good driver. But if someone cut me off, blocked me from changing lanes in order to exit, honked their bloody horn at me (just because I was following a wee bit too close) or anything else that felt like an attack on my manhood, I would whip out my middle finger while slamming the horn and yelling obscenities that, fortunately, only I could hear. I began my recovery from road rage by creating affirmations that described the driver I wished to become, such as:

"When someone cuts me off in traffic, I remain calm, react quickly and take steps to maintain control."

"I understand that everyone makes mistakes."

"When facing danger on the road, I remain calm and effective."

To speed up the process, I flooded my subconscious with affirmations. This was my program:

1. I wrote my affirmations every day, once in first person (I, Steve, am a peaceful and skilled defensive driver), and once in second person (Steve is a peaceful and skilled defensive driver). I used both voices because some beliefs begin as statements made by others and some as conclusions we make from personal experimentation.
2. I read my affirmations first thing in the morning and again just before falling asleep.
3. I recorded my affirmations with inspirational music in the background. I would listen to each one three

times in first person and three times in second person, leaving enough space between to repeat them back. I would play this recording whenever I was in my car and, as a real estate salesperson, that was often.
4. I also made the same recording in a soft voice with peaceful music. This one I played at night, using a pillow speaker or earbuds, absorbing the messages all night long.
5. I also spent a few minutes each day in a quiet space, closing my eyes and picturing myself in various traffic situations, responding as if my desired behavior was already a reality.

Within a few weeks, I noticed a change in how I responded in traffic. I had retired my middle finger and probably lowered my blood pressure by several points. It was a great affirmation that imagery could be used to alter behavior efficiently!

I also discovered through this experiment and other experiences that some of what I had learned was seminar garbage and needed to be tossed out. I realized that some (though not all) trainers oversimplify a process so that it is more marketable. For instance, I had read/heard that I could change any habit in 21 days or 30 days, depending on the trainer—sound familiar? If you have heard these or any other "magic" time frames, they are about as useful as a steering wheel on a dirt bike.

The truth, in my experience, is that a habit or belief of any kind can be changed in an instant, a week, month, year or perhaps never. The time it takes to alter a habit depends on many factors: your desire to change, your belief in your ability to change, how many and how strong the conflicting old beliefs, and your commitment to diligently work the transformation process, just to list a few. In general, I recommend a healthy level of skepticism when it comes to personal growth trainers—including me. If you are drawn to a philosophy or program, experiment with it, test it out. If it works, great. If not, eject and keep searching.

Having altered my driving behavior, I was ready to climb out of the deep, dark, depressing hole I had lived in for most of my life. I created a long list of affirmations about my impressive speaking abilities—gulp. Scared the hell out of me.

What my outer self believed at that time was that I would look and sound terrified, that as I began to speak my brain would freeze along with the rest of me. I saw the audience laughing at my embarrassing display. But I spent weeks repeating the same process I used to adjust my driving attitude: writing, reading, recording and listening to my affirmations. Like with the students shooting free throws, I would trick my subconscious into believing I could speak to large groups of people—without throwing up, hopefully.

Next, I had to create a reason why a group would invite me to speak to them, so I wrote an article, titled *White Knight Syndrome*, which appeared in a nationally distributed magazine. A week or so after publication I received a call from the Sacramento Board of Realtors asking me to speak about my article at an upcoming meeting. They expected about 300 people. Before I could faint, I accepted their invitation, hung up the phone, then fainted. I was terrified. I had a couple of weeks for my affirmations to kick in. I began thinking of ways out of my commitment. I could tell them I had laryngitis or a touch of leprosy. I could move out of the state, change my name, or move to Lodi and do whatever they do in Lodi. I could rob a 7-Eleven and get arrested. While these alternatives were tempting, I was determined to see my experiment through to the end.

The day before the event, I checked into a hotel near the meeting hall and frantically stalked the room reading my affirmations off a pile of 3x5 cards. The next morning, I considered driving to Tahoe, scoring big at blackjack and buying a mobile taco truck. Instead, I showed up, stood before the group, gave my speech, did not freeze, did not throw up on myself and even received some polite applause. I'm sure my presentation was less than stellar, but I did it!

What I've discovered since this initial experiment in transformation is that moving an activity out of the fearful, "I'll never go there" zone into the comfort zone is a two-part process:

1. Using visualization weakens the fear, casts some doubt on the old limiting beliefs and allows one to act—not perfectly and not without anxiety, but act.
2. Then, by continuing to act, the experience and positive feedback received strengthens the new, more powerful, more productive belief.

SUPERPOWER SUMMARY

> The SuperPower you are invited to liberate here is the commitment, passion and willingness to change your world by changing yourself. The problem with changing where you work, where you live or what career you pursue is that it can prevent you from effecting real, lasting change—change that can only come from within.
>
> Become the change you wish to manifest and you will attract everything you need to make it so.

CHAPTER 2

THE POWER OF PERSONAL RESPONSIBILITY

> SUPERPOWER:
> By accepting responsibility for your life up to now, you empower yourself to mold your life going forward.

Google *personal responsibility* and you will find a variety of definitions, most of which appear to be synonymous with *blame*—"You have to take responsibility for your mess!" Assigning responsibility, however, is not the same as blame. Blame is a judgment after the fact, a witch hunt, the pointing of fingers. Taking responsibility is a way of approaching life. Whether or not you are taking responsibility for your experiences during this lifetime can be determined by answering one simple question: **Who is steering my boat?**

Victims might say that the current location and condition of their boat is the result of a strong wind, the changing tides, or perhaps being sideswiped by someone else's boat. They believe their experiences are the result of external causes—people and circumstances beyond their control.

Self-directed people would acknowledge the wind, the tide and the errant boat, but attribute the location and condition of the boat to how they chose to turn the wheel, rig the sails, and respond to threats like swerving to avoid an imminent collision. They know that their experience is based on their *response* to what they observe in the world—not the object of their observation.

So, how does this understanding of self-responsibility relate to this quote: "*Beliefs* are the determinants of what one experiences. There are no external causes."–David Hawkins, internationally renowned psychiatrist, physician, researcher

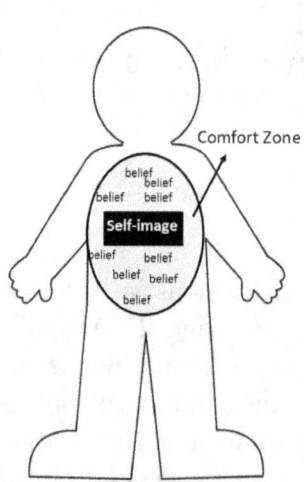

Our *responses* to external stimuli are based on the database of *beliefs* we store in our comfort zones. If we *believe* polar bears are dangerous, when we encounter one on the street, we run. So, what personal responsibility comes down to is: *You* making decisions as to which beliefs *you* will accept and store in your comfort zone and which you will reject—*you* decide, not your parents, not your boss, not your favorite celebrity or blogger. Yes, a parent may have told you that you're lazy—but it is up to you to accept that judgment or toss it aside. Understanding the relationship between **what you believe** and **what you experience** is fundamental to your ability to liberate and employ your SuperPowers to live a happy, healthy, fulfilling and prosperous life—so let's get into it.

You can think of the beliefs stored in your comfort zone as the charts you rely upon to navigate the river of life. The charts contain all of the rules you've selected—rules that you believe will keep you safe and secure. The comfort zone is a model of life that you create—a place where you think you can live in comfort with minimal pain and anxiety.

There are many types of beliefs within your comfort zone—rules representing your understanding of how the world works, how you should interact with the world to evoke minimal pain, how you avoid danger and who you believe you are. At the center of your belief system is your self-image. It consists of all of your beliefs about who you are—your most precious, core beliefs.

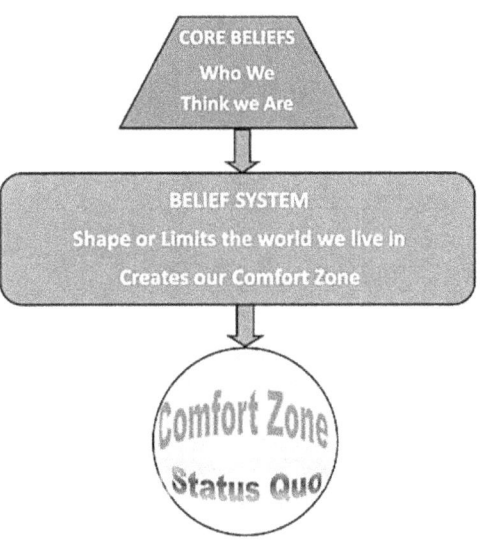

Core values are foundational—the beliefs you hold most dear, what you believe are immutable truths. Out of all the limitless possibilities, they are fundamental convictions you have chosen—truths you believe about yourself, beginning in childhood. Your core values provide the criteria for accepting or rejecting other beliefs that populate your database.

If your abusive father gets drunk regularly and calls you worthless, you might believe the unenlightened Neanderthal. This core belief could lead to new opinions like, "I don't need to go to college; I'm never going to amount to anything anyway" or "I'll never convince a good, self-respecting woman to marry me, so why try?"

Because the world you see/experience is based on what you choose to believe, managing your stored beliefs is key to creating the life of your dreams. So, let's take this chapter to understand this miraculous process and how you can access it, on-demand, as you uncover and engage your inner SuperPowers.

Since all that you experience with your senses and all the resultant feelings and emotions are based on what you have chosen to believe about yourself—the world around you and how you can interact with that world—it seems important to understand how you created this comfort zone and populated it with thousands of beliefs.

In the Beginning—Populating Your Comfort Zone with a Belief System

Your "comfort zone" is where you store all the beliefs that make up your unique model of the world—as unique as the complex mix of experiences you have encountered. It is an idyllic, self-selected world in which you believe you can live securely with minimal risk of pain and minimal anxiety. I call it Disney World, the happiest place on earth, where the boat you're navigating down the river of life runs on steel tracks and the mechanical hippos never eat your fingers, even if you cover them in peanut butter and dangle them into the water. Like Disney World, your artificial, internal model of the world is a fantasy.

You began accumulating your unique set of beliefs the moment you entered this world. These can be as basic as "fire burns" or as complex as prejudicial beliefs toward groups of people: the Irish drink whiskey, Germans drink beer, English drink warm beer, Russians drink vodka, and college students drink… anything. Some beliefs are based on personal experience, like touching fire. Stored belief: Fire burns—don't touch! Other opinions are referral: Your dad tells you that people with money are not to be trusted, probably because he never had much. You are six years old and trust your dad implicitly, so you store a belief that causes you to avoid and distrust wealthy people. You also avoid becoming wealthy yourself because you would never want to be seen as untrustworthy. Thanks a lot, Dad!

The hunt for your hidden SuperPowers begins with this understanding: Your unique collection of beliefs create your experience of the world. The difference between deliberate, self-directed people and everyone else is that self-directed people understand this process and consciously monitor and manage their beliefs so that they support their goals. How can you maintain your collected beliefs so that they remain in alignment with your goals? To answer this question, examine how and why you've selected and managed your beliefs up to now.

According to BabyCenter.com, as a newborn, you had no sense of yourself as an individual: You thought that you and your mom were one. You didn't realize that the tiny hands and feet waving before you were your own. You were born a beautiful, pristine blank slate — no fear, no sense of limitation, one with everything. Your ego, or comfort zone, was an empty shell. Ah, but we

know what the Universe does with empty vessels, don't we? It fills them. With what? With cupcakes and crap—whatever we "believe to be true." The process looks something like this:

In the beginning, you are one with the Mother. You're in and of her body. Your body draws from her nutrients and cells to grow. You are one person expanding its presence. Then one day you are rudely tugged out of your extended body and thrust into the cold, dry air of reality by a funny-looking creature in a green smock, hat and mask. But still, you have no sense of separateness. You believe that you are one with everything. You have no limitations. Infinite possibilities abound.

Once on the outside of the "big body," you become the subject of the good opinions of others—most of whom have something to say OUT LOUD about who you are and who or what you should become. It begins with a lot of strangers telling you how precious 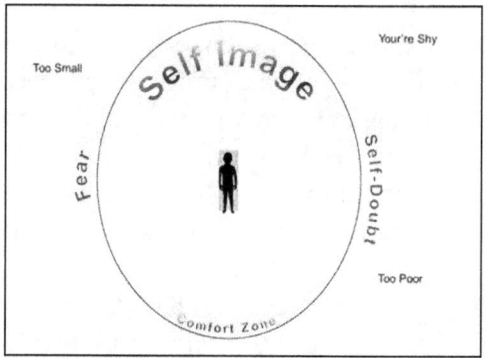 and adorable you are. But then you also hear things like, "He is so shy" or "What a small baby" or "Too bad she was born into such a poor family" or "Is that his nose or is he sucking on a cucumber?" This is the beginning of the construction of the self-image.

As you grow, you are exposed to more opinions from parents, friends, teachers, television, movies, magazines, etc. **You do have a choice of which ideas you believe.** However, children are highly susceptible to the views of influential people like parents, teachers and friends. The more prominent the person, the more likely you

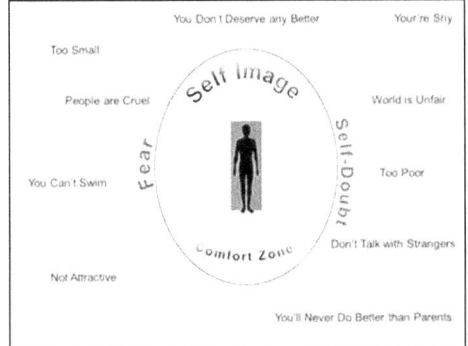

are to add their opinions to your system of beliefs. That's why parents get the brunt of the blame for "making us who we are." They are the most influential people in our lives and the ones with whom we spend the most time during our susceptible years. Ultimately, however, it is your responsibility to judge the truth of what you hear, then incorporate it into your belief system or reject it.

You arrive at adulthood with a full-blown self-image, a well-defined comfort zone filled with rules about life and how you need to interact with it. These rules make up your belief system—everything you think you "know" about life—what you can and can't do, what you like and don't like, what hurts and what nourishes, what is dangerous and what is safe. It's the job of your comfort zone to guide you to experiences that will support the person you think you are and to protect you from experiences that do not support that image.

The Dragon Cage

Mythologist Joseph Campbell referred to the self-image as the "dragon cage." And this cage, in mythological terms, is guarded

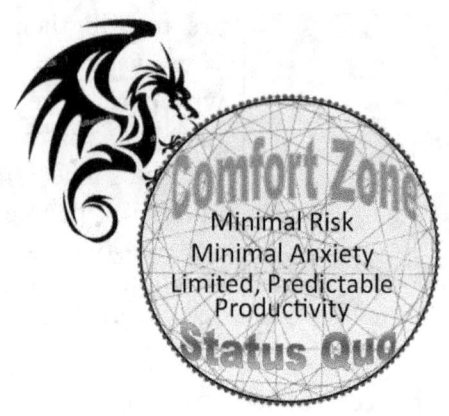

by a dragon. A fundamental question for self-directed people to ask themselves is: "Will I remain inside the cage and live a small, secure life with minimal risk of pain and anxiety, or will I face the dragon—escape the lure of security for an expansive, adventurous life?"

The decision is entirely up to you—not an easy one for most of us. The cage is comfortable—that's why it is called the comfort zone, duh. You store all the things you "know" to be true within the zone. And "knowing" makes you feel secure, gives you that warm, dull glow in the pit of your stomach.

A downside to living a small, secure life within the cage is that you don't "know" how the world works and how you should interact with it. You think you know based on very, very limited exposure to the world (let me add two more: very, very). You selected the beliefs, stored within your dragon cage, based on a minuscule number of experiences compared with the endless parade of life assaulting your senses at any given time. Not to mention those in every other region of the world that you will never visit.

A person who lives their entire life in West Overshoe, Wisconsin is doomed to experience mostly those things they have absorbed from the West Overshoe culture. Take a single issue like what to eat. In West Overshoe, it's gravy. Everything that can be baked, broiled, boiled, sautéed, tossed or barbecued gets slathered with thick, greasy, salty, tasty gravy. Contrast this to the nearly infinite variety of foods throughout the world. If our West Overshoer takes a rare vacation to Japan and asks for gravy on his sushi, he is liable to experience the sharp end of a sashimi blade. The point is: because you've based your beliefs on such narrow, limited experiences, they are continually challenged, flatly rejected and frequently wrong—a poorly constructed, inaccurate wall separating your expectations from reality.

Another downside to living within the limits of your self-imposed world is that researchers in the Psychology of Human Productivity have found that remaining within the comfort zone results in predictably limited productivity. Makes sense, right? No risk, no reward.

Escape or Expand your Dragon Cage

One alternative, if you are bored with the status quo of your comfort zone is 'the breakout.' While they can work, breakouts are not for the faint of heart. Escaping your comfort zone, acting in ways that are out of sync with your limiting beliefs, can be scary, stressful and short-lived. If you have a fear of human interaction but a desire to eat and pay the mortgage, you can suck-it-up and force yourself to make sales calls. But don't think you're fooling anyone. Your prospective customers will pick up on your anxiety, fear and self-doubt. There are also health issues created by living with too much stress.

Fortunately, there is an alternative to an outright breakout. I have personally found that I am far more likely to expand my world if I can do it while retaining a certain level of comfort. I'm not a masochist, after all! To that end, I decided to expand my comfort zone so that, long-term, the activities required of a new goal would become part of my comfortable world.

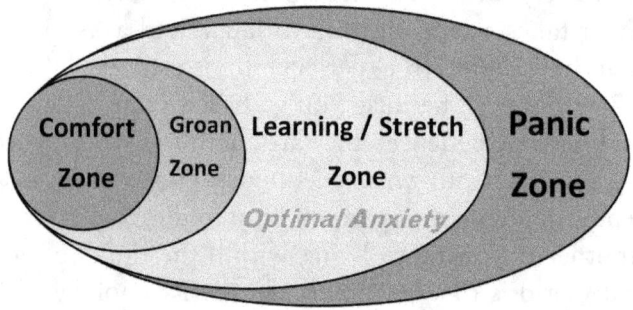

Researchers, looking for ways to increase the efficacy of people in the workplace, found that they could improve productivity by getting people to stretch beyond their comfort levels—but not too far beyond. If they extended past the **groan zone,** to the stretch or **learning zone,** it created an **Optimal Anxiety.** They were uncomfortable, but not so much so that they were unwilling to go there. If they spent enough time in the stretch zone, those nervous activities eventually became integrated into their comfort zones—improving their productivity and reducing stress. If the researchers made them stretch too far, beyond the groan and stretch zones into the panic zone, their anxiety levels would provoke a rapid retreat back to the known. In this case, productivity would suffer. It's like an out-of-shape athlete turned couch potato who decides to run a marathon. If she starts by jogging a few blocks, then slowly increases her speed and distance, she will eventually be ready for the marathon. If she were to try to run a half-marathon on day one, without any preparation, the agony and pain would probably have her retreating to the couch with a handful of Advil.

The Source of Suffering

It is ironic that the cage you built and the dragon you conceived to protect it so that you would feel safe and secure are the very things that give rise to pain and suffering. Within your comfort zone, you've created the image of a perfect world, a world which does not exist. The real world, by comparison, will almost always come up short—thus internal conflict and suffering. Not the best plan for living a happy, healthy, prosperous life. We are such silly little creatures. Years ago, Dan Milman, who wrote *Way of the Peaceful Warrior*, told me that **all suffering is caused by seeing life the way it is and wishing it were some other way**—the way we expect it to be, based on our belief system. It is our resistance to unexpected and unwanted reality that causes so much pain in our lives. This understanding is the basis of much of the teaching in the Buddhist tradition.

So, if your database of beliefs can cause so much suffering, why do you need it? We evolved this memory storage system as a way to process the massive amount of data assaulting our senses which, unabated, would cause our brains to figuratively, if not literally, explode. Fortunately, we also evolved a way of using the beliefs stored in our comfort zones to process this data-storm and prevent exploding our brains.

The mechanism that links our beliefs to what we experience was described in 1960 when Dr. Maxwell Maltz published *Psycho-Cybernetics*. This groundbreaking work gave us a better understanding of Ralph Waldo Emerson's assertion that "We are what we think about all day long." Dr. Maltz said: "Your **Automatic Creative Mechanism** is teleological: it operates in terms of goals and end results. Once you give it a definite goal to achieve, you can depend upon its automatic guidance system to guide you to that goal much better than you ever could by conscious thought alone."

You supply the goal by focusing on results. Your automatic mechanism then provides the means. Whether Dr. Maltz realized it or not, the Automatic Creative Mechanism he described is what we know of as the Reticular Activating System, or RAS.

Simply stated, the Reticular Formation is a network of nerves at your brainstem that **filters out unnecessary information so that the relevant stuff gets through.**

To better understand this critical internal process, let's take a quick look at the RAS, why you need it and how it interacts with your belief system to help you achieve anything you desire.

Every day your senses are bombarded with stimuli—sights, sounds, tastes, touch, environmental conditions, feelings, concepts, opinions. If you had to analyze every bit of data that crosses your field of awareness, you would be in constant overwhelm—your brain would explode. After about 150 research studies, there is some agreement that the unconscious mind is bombarded with about 11 million bits-per-second of raw data from all our senses. But the conscious mind cannot process more than 40 bits-per-second and is typically only handling roughly 16 bits-per-second. So, what happens to the other 10,999,960 bits-per-second that never make it into our conscious awareness?

1. Filter in—Filter out: The RAS dampens and tamps down the effects of repeated stimuli such as loud noises, helping to prevent the senses from being overloaded. It compares your wants, needs, beliefs and expectations with the data flowing into your mind and ignores anything that is not currently relevant to your life while tuning in to information you need to Survive or Thrive. A classic example of this is a new mother who can sleep through loud city traffic but is awakened promptly by the sound of her crying baby in a closed nursery down the hallway.

    When my girls were babies it seemed like I saw Huggies and Love's diaper commercials every time I turned on the TV—they were relevant to my life. I guess they went out of business because I swear I haven't seen a diaper commercial since the girls graduated to "big girl pants." Once they became irrelevant, diapers seemingly became invisible. Works for me.

2. Autopilot: By pre-judging relevant information from this massive data-storm, we catalog preprogrammed responses so that future encounters require little or no thought. When you encounter a new experience, you analyze, experiment and decide how to best interact during this and future meetings. You store this decision in your belief

system, in your comfort zone, so that the next time you encounter this or similar experiences, no experimentation is required—you merely respond based on your prior, memorized decision. If you pet a strange dog and get bit, you store a belief that strange dogs are dangerous—avoid! Without this saved belief, you would experiment over and over until you run out of fingers. Armed with this automatic response, when you come across future strange dogs, you don't have to think twice. Your eyes alert your RAS to the fact that a dog is approaching. It compares this data with the contents of your belief system. If it finds a belief that dogs are dangerous, you cross the street—that is, unless you receive new information that causes you to modify this belief.

The good news is that your beliefs are not static. If they were, you could use this book as kindling. You don't have to hold onto beliefs that are so far from reality that they limit or diminish your experience of life. Throughout your life, you have the choice of adding to, deleting or modifying beliefs based on new input. A chance, positive encounter with a strange dog might prompt you to alter your opinion to "Some strange dogs are dangerous and some are friendly—approach with caution and an open mind."

An early human, being chased by a rival, comes across an apple tree. He picks up a handful of apples from the ground and throws them at his pursuer, who runs away. The man makes a mental note and adds it to his list of beliefs: "Apples make great weapons." Hungry, and attracted by the smell of the crushed apples, he licks his fingers. Yummy. His belief is now modified:

"Apples can be weapons or yummy applesauce." Note to self: When being pursued by a large predator, don't throw applesauce. The construction of your belief system is a lifelong process, a new development at first, followed by continuous modification.

The RAS filter compares the things you desire to your values and beliefs and determines whether they are congruent. Does the item you want reflect and support the person you think you are? Or do you have beliefs that would prevent you from obtaining this object of your desire? If it turns out that the desired object is not congruent with what you believe, you have two choices, unless you want to have a boatload of stress raining down on your head: You can forget about your goal or you can modify your belief. If, on the other hand, you find congruency, your request will be passed on to your brain, altering your perception to bring focus onto anything or anyone who could help you achieve this want or need. In high school when a pretty girl asked me out, confronted with how I felt about my physical appearance, I begged off. Had I been aware of the process we're discussing, I could have revised how I felt about my appearance and maybe had a date or two before turning 18. Would've been nice!

Pretty slick, don't you think? Huge. Armed with this knowledge, you can program your senses to tune into anything in your environment that will help you achieve goals congruent with your evolving self-image.

You will never have the power to change your life for the better if you do not accept responsibility for the choices that led to your current life experience.

If our Superpowers are hidden, who hid them? At first I thought it was my parents, then I suspected my ex-wives in collusion, then my ex-bosses; the list goes on and on. Eventually I realized that there was no one to blame, not even me. It turns out I didn't have to search for my powers at all. All I had to do was take responsibility and acknowledge that I had hidden them, buried them in self-doubt and my belief in limitations.

The unique path that is your life is the product of millions of choices, small choices like coffee or tea, and meaningful choices like career and marriage. If you would like to access your inner powers to assist you in living a happy, productive, prosperous life, you must assume full responsibility for every choice you have made thus far, and every decision you will make going forward.

SUPERPOWER SUMMARY

Your experience of the world is determined by the beliefs you've chosen to catalog in your memory—beliefs about who you are, how the world works and how you can best interact with the world. Accepting responsibility for the beliefs that molded your life up to now, and for all future beliefs, is a SuperPower you will need to access if you choose to take control of your life and move it in the direction of your dreams.

The Power to choose and direct your life path is rooted in this understanding. Reject that responsibility and your life becomes a game of paddleball—and guess who gets to be the ball? Accept responsibility for your life up to now and you empower yourself to mold your life going forward.

CHAPTER 3

THE POWER OF USING YOUR FEAR TO CHANGE YOUR LIFE

SUPERPOWER:
The ability to get off your butt and commit—commit to ending unnecessary suffering, to using fear as a tool instead of letting it use you.

Just because you decided in Chapter 1 to create a happier, more fulfilling and prosperous life doesn't mean that you won't experience fear and anxiety along the way. Change is inevitable but scary, so understanding how to work with and control fear is essential.

When I began my real estate sales career, I was terrified. The first thing my manager told me to do was call for-sale-by-owners (FSBOs, pronounced Fizzboze) and convince them to list their homes with me. I later learned that very few agents could tolerate the abuse they assumed would befall them if they approached FSBOs. I would be yelled at, scorned and perhaps even physically assaulted. But I had made my choice to do whatever it took to conquer my fear of human interaction. If this is what it took, I would do it.

I'd like to say that I heroically conquered my fear and boldly made my phone calls, asking for appointments. Truth is, I called from home, sitting in a dim room with a glass of Boone's Farm Strawberry Hill in one hand, a joint in one hand and the phone in… Well, you get the picture. Hey, it's a process. I'm not particularly proud of and would not necessarily recommend the get-high-to-call technique but, for me, it worked. Since then I have replaced the wine and joint with affirmations and acceptance—much better for your liver and lungs, and more effective.

Fear in our society is mostly seen as a roadblock

DANGER! Don't go this way! Keep out! Attack Cat! Trespassers shall be arrested, reported, towed, shot, fined and eaten! Big cat!

Fear is fundamentally a signpost designating an area of uncertainty: STOP! DANGER! It alerts us whenever we're about to travel from the known to the unknown. It is a by-product of our beliefs—an enforcement tool we utilize whenever our RAS finds a conflict between what we believe and what the world is asking of us—the wall we construct that blocks access to any place, person or situation that is outside of our self-constructed, limiting comfort zone.

Fear does not exist in nature. Tattoo this on your forehead ASAP— the color of ink, your call. Very important. There is no such phenomenon in the universe except within our imaginations. So stop thinking of fear as a big, dark monster lurking around every corner.

If I believe that I am a great swimmer, will I feel fear at the prospect of getting into a friend's backyard pool? Of course not.

But if I firmly believe that I cannot swim, that I will sink like a rock in any water deeper than 5'8" (my height), you can bet I am going to conjure up a fear response to keep my body on dry land.

My fear of swimming protects and perpetuates the belief that I cannot swim—an impression I was given by my dad who told my brother and me that the men in our family have some rare "specific gravity" that causes us to sink rather than float. I think that means we're dense. That was, of course, crap—my dad's way of rationalizing his fear of water. But, as discussed, I was a kid, he was my dad—so I don't swim.

Another example: A young man wants to pursue a career in law enforcement. He is going to school, working a full-time job, paying all his expenses and having a hard time getting by. He's in a grocery store and notices that no one is watching him just as his eyes lock onto a package of amazing-looking tenderloins. He salivates at the thought of eating beef without two buns, ketchup and a bag of fries. As he goes to jam the fillets into his shorts, his stomach turns sour, his heart beats rapidly, and his skin turns cold and clammy. He returns the beef to the display case.

This is an excellent illustration of a belief system in action. Two beliefs dissuade our cop from larceny. The first is part of his chosen self-image as an honest person who does not steal from others. The second is his vision of becoming a law enforcement officer. When he closes his eyes, he can see himself in a dark blue uniform, shiny badge and, of course, his very own Glock 19. This vision does not include a package of tenderloins protruding from his utility belt. He is suddenly afraid of the consequences a criminal record might have on his future career. His fear has helped him to move, unimpeded, along his chosen path. See, who said fear couldn't be a friend?

Note that, in both examples, it is not the circumstance that causes us to access our fear response; it is the conflict between the event and one or more beliefs.

Some fears keep you safe, like the fear of growling dogs. Others motivate you, like a fear of poverty. These fear markers keep you moving safely along your life path.

Some fears, however, restrict life unnecessarily. They don't facilitate progress as much as they impede. While my fear of water protects my old belief that I can't swim, that belief is based on bad information. The fear block is preventing me from enjoying the water—swimming, snorkeling, scuba, time with friends.

When you feel your stomach twisting into a knot, a pressure in your head and an urge to find the nearest bathroom, how do you know if the fear you are experiencing is helpful, even essential, to your survival—or if it is limiting your experience, holding you back from enjoying life to its fullest?

First, be aware of the fear, and curious about its origin and purpose.

If I accept, even defend, my fear of water as "just part of who I am," I avoid getting into deep water. If, as a self-directed person, I recognize that I have based my fear of water on a bonehead belief my Dad passed on to me, I can address that belief head-on. I can weaken it with a variety of visualization techniques until I am comfortable jumping into the pool, perhaps take lessons and eventually winning six Olympic Gold medals or whatever.

You can choose to remain within your self-constructed prison, cowering from imaginary walls of fear, or you can transform the walls into thin, penetrable rice paper.

How to Transform your Relationship with Fear

Remember why you create your fears—to block you from going where you believe you should not or cannot go—to feel safe and secure within the world of your creation, a world where you think you 'know' the rules of the game.

Imagine being raised in a small town. You were taught from birth that life outside your village was fraught with danger and that the only safe path would be to find work and a suitable local mate and settle down for a lifetime within the town limits. What imaginary fears might you construct to keep yourself at home? Fear of crime in the "big city," fear of people with different colored skin or accents, fear of being discriminated against as an uneducated yokel who only has sex with farm animals? It doesn't matter if your rationalizations are valid or even reasonable. All that matters is that you believe them to justify your limited life experience.

If you learn to accept or even welcome the unexpected, you reduce the reasons for constructing fear borders.

While you can temporarily weaken a fear response with visualizations and affirmations (enough to dip your toe in the water), lasting relief comes from transforming your relationship with fear—becoming more accepting of change, more willing to enter the unknown with curiosity.

As I often urge my students, fall out of love with your beliefs. Remember that they are not necessarily accurate or helpful to your life. They are just judgments that you have etched into your memory. Reject your need for security, which Helen Keller discovered does not even exist in our world. Be open to a surprising, adventurous future.

Be willing to move through your life story without knowing the entire plot up front or how it will end. (I can tell you—spoiler alert—that you're going to die. Get over it.) I mean, what the hell! Who is to say that the story you've created in your head is the best you can do? As far as I know, we get one shot at happiness and fulfillment on the planet. With endless possibilities, why limit yourself to life within a carefully constructed prison cell? Why not at least weaken the bars enough to allow for occasional spontaneous breakouts?

Make Fear Your Buddy

Another way to become less of a slave to fear is to develop a conscious relationship with it. Talk with fear as if it was another person. You can even name it—let's use Seymour.

"Thank you, Seymour. I appreciate that you made me pee myself to keep me from raising my hand to go to the restroom. However, we need to talk about this fear of talking with strangers. It was useful when I was five, walking home from school—you kept me safe, and I do appreciate that. But now I'm a thirty-year-old real estate agent going broke because I'm afraid to speak to strangers about selling their homes. Time for an adjustment, dude."

This may sound silly to you, but try it. And remember, fear is not a real thing; it doesn't exist in nature. It is you. It is your way of protecting yourself when you've decided you need protection. No more than that.

Now that you and Seymour are getting tight, notice how you become increasingly aware of his presence. Something doesn't work out the way you want or expect, and the inner trash talk begins. *Why did I say that? I'm sure my client is going to kill the sale now, which means no mortgage payment next month. I may even have to start drinking cheap wine, God forbid!* When life fails to meet our expectations, we tend to snap to negative, insecure thinking. Unchecked, negative, fear-based thoughts can spiral out of control, leaving us agitated, in no position to take command of the situation and solve the problem.

The solution to this downward spiral is to listen to the conversation you're having with Seymour before it gains too much momentum.

1. Recognize it for what it is—*you* talking to *you* in a manner that you have decided. *You* are Seymour's scriptwriter. Heck, you're Seymour!
2. Ask yourself: Does this dialog serve me—does it help the others involved?
3. If you intercept and control this conversation quickly enough, it puts you in charge of your emotions, rather than the other way around. Not that you need to become a zombie, devoid of emotion. If you want to get pissed, rant and rave, go for it. At least make it a conscious decision and not a preprogrammed, negative and unproductive robo-response.

Don't Sleep with Fear

You get an email just before going to bed. Your boss wants to see you first thing in the morning. You wake up in the middle of the night running all kinds of negative, fear-based scenarios: "I'm getting demoted. Worse, I'm getting fired. Sheila in accounting has filed a sexual harassment complaint. No, wait, Sheila's my wife, she wouldn't do that. I'm probably getting fired." You start making mental lists of what you will do depending on which disaster occurs and another list of the bills you won't be able to pay once you're fired. How long before the dealer impounds your car and Sheila files for divorce? You are on a downward spiral—mourning a series of calamities, none of which have happened and probably never will.

At times like this, I recommend that you jump out of bed and kick Seymour's ass. Recognize that you are creating the runaway negative thoughts. Talk with yourself: *There I go again, letting my negativity bias get the best of me, worrying about something that hasn't even happened and probably never will. The boss is as likely to give me a promotion or a raise.* Choose to replace fear and doubt with faith that it will all work out—one way or another.

If there are actions you want to take the next day, write them down in your bedside notebook or record them with a bedside mini-recorder or smartphone recording app. Then, go back to bed and change the subject. Fear tends to lead us into ever-shrinking tunnels of myopic thinking. Focus on some other area of your life until you fall back to sleep—an upcoming vacation, fun hikes you have planned for the weekend. Remind yourself of how much more expansive your life is beyond income and bills. It can also help to suspend *me* focus. Reach out to someone you know in need. Cheer up a friend. Volunteer to do some work for a local charity. Serve lunch at a soup kitchen.

When I feel myself spiraling down in a fear block, I remind myself to keep fearful thoughts in perspective:

1. In 110 years, everyone currently on earth will be gone—replaced by an entirely new world population. How important is the fact that I lost my phone?

2. In 30 years, I'll be gone from the planet. And when I go, my in-basket will still be full; my credit cards will have balances due; and in the refrigerator, tubs of yogurt will be way past their expiration date.

There is no end game, just an end. No perfect destination on the planet only an unknown number of days and then an inevitable departure. Sorry, but there it is. How long you live is not nearly as important as how well. Look at some very accomplished people who died young but contributed much: James Dean, 24; Nathan Hale, 21; Jean Harlow, 26; John Keats 25; Robert Johnson, 27; Amy Weinhouse, 27; Tupac Shakur, 25; Heath Ledger, 28. Do you have time to waste getting freaked out because your boss wants to see you in the morning? Even if you experience your worst fear and are fired, how many of your limited number of days are you willing to waste worrying about it? Especially when you know that your next job will likely lead to new, exciting experiences. It may be where you meet the love of your life, experience great fulfillment and earn mucho bucks. So many times I have experienced changes that I thought were the end of the line for me, only to find that further down the line was a pot of gold.

Go on a Fear Reduction Campaign

A long-term, deeply embedded fear may be too resistant to the simple realization of its existence and your desire to eliminate it. You may need to go through a process of reducing the fear by altering the underlying belief *it* is protecting. If I don't want to feel fear every time I'm asked to go swimming, I could work on my feeling that I can't swim. Create affirmations about what a good swimmer I am, take lessons… Once the belief is modified or deleted, the fear response disappears.

I used to have a fear of heights that kept me from enjoying much of life. I remember when I was a teenager, my dad lined up a summer job for me, preparing two homes for full exterior painting. They both needed to have the old flaking paint scraped and sanded. This, to my great disappointment, required standing on a ladder, two stories in the air, overlooking Boulder Creek. Dang, double fear: I was afraid of heights and I couldn't swim. But I needed the money to supplement my band income—back then we were lucky to get paid $100 per gig, split five ways. Beer money.

So that's how I spent that hot Boulder summer, clinging to a ladder with one hand, scraping paint with the other and sweating suntan lotion into my eyes. Terrifying. In my thirties, I decided that I was no longer willing to limit my life to activities I could accomplish within 5'8" of ground level. I began by using the techniques I had learned from Shakti Gawain. I imagined that I was comfortable with heights. I wrote, read and listened to affirmations until I was confident enough to begin exploring heights, spending time on ladders, eventually riding roller coasters. I also focused on accepting all results. Yes, I could fall, break something or even die—but probably not. It's not like I should expect to live an adventurous life without ever breaking a bone, and I sure can't expect to live forever. Within a few weeks, I transformed my fear to excitement. I even came to enjoy roller coasters and have ridden some of the highest and fastest in the world. My life partner, Gina, and I have a phrase we use when one of us is succumbing to fear: "You'll be dead soon!" Some of my students find this morbid. I find it to be a very positive and motivational thought. If you kid yourself into believing you'll live a long life, you have all the time in the world to get it right. "I'll work on fear later when I have the time." When you realize that time is short and could end today, doing what it takes to feel happy and fulfilled moves to the top of your list of priorities.

The planet doesn't care whether you spend your life in fear, worry and debt, or in harmony, love and prosperity. In the end, it will take back your molecules and energy whether you had a happy, loving life or one of suffering. Taking your licks doesn't even buy you an extra hour on the planet. No points for martyrdom. May as well be happy and relatively free of fear.

If you think you would prefer peace and joy over suffering in fear, when will you make that choice? When will your actions reflect that choice? What are you waiting for?

SUPERPOWER SUMMARY

> Instead of blindly following fearful thoughts down the rabbit hole, remind yourself that they are self-created and, therefore, can be modified or rejected by you. What you have the power to create, you have the power to modify or delete.
>
> The SuperPower you are offered in this chapter is the ability to get off your butt and commit—commit to ending unnecessary suffering, to using fear as a tool instead of letting it use you, to clearing away self-imposed obstructions and moving your life in the direction of your dreams.

CHAPTER 4

THE POWER TO CONTROL JUDGMENT

> **SUPERPOWER:**
> Learn when to rely on autopilot and when to shut it off. When you replace knowing with sincere curiosity, you see the real, complex person, not the judgment.

"We judge people for judging people because judging people is wrong." —Anonymous (funny person, that Anonymous)

In Chapter 1, I described the stored belief system, which resides in your comfort zone. These beliefs comprise your outer self-image: who you think you are, how the world functions, and how you and the world should interact. The opinions you store about the world and how you interact with it are essential due to your limited capacity to process data. They allow you to respond automatically to thousands of situations you encounter regularly. They also help you to focus on what is important and sensitize your perception to information that will help you succeed.

The Downside of Stored Beliefs

Even though a stored belief system is critical to your capacity to process data and maintain sanity, it has a significant, potentially disastrous side effect—judgment!

After getting bit by a strange dog, you might decide that dogs are dangerous and should be avoided. While this might prevent future teeth-to-leg contact, it will also deprive you and a lot of friendly dogs of the joy of petting, being pet and an occasional face lick.

Problems arise when you rely on your stored beliefs in more complex situations—like when encountering other humans.

Our ability to store beliefs and use them to categorize and deal with objects and situations quickly is so efficient and convenient that it can easily be over-utilized. If you are assaulted by an Eskimo while attempting to sell him ice cubes at an elevated price, you may store a belief that Eskimos are rude and dangerous—avoid. In the future, you will evade Eskimos. If an Eskimo family wants to move into your co op, you might plot to derail their application and freeze them out (pun intended). If you are a landlord, you might invent excuses why you cannot rent to those blubber-eating, nose-rubbing igloo-dwellers. This is the root of prejudice or discrimination and is, of course, hurtful, unfair and, in some cases, illegal—stupidity born of ignorance. Harmful judgments are often the result of accepting discriminatory beliefs by referral. If your swastika-tattooed, Confederate flag-waving, skinhead uncle raises you, you just might pick up some tendencies toward bigotry. Whether you then become bigoted is, of course, your choice.

We may, at times, rely on a belief to judge and label situations and objects that are too complex to be stereotyped. In other words, we get it wrong or, at least, incomplete. In the words of Søren Kierkegaard, the famed Danish theologian:

"Once you label me, you negate me."

A later version of this quote, from Wayne Dyer, is one of my favorites:

"When you label me, you limit me."

We label everything and everyone to maintain sanity in the face of chaos. Labeling organizes and simplifies our lives. It also reduces our understanding of people to superficial archetypes. We judge the whole, complicated individual based on one isolated event, one small aspect of who they are. I hear it all the time: "She's stupid—doesn't know anything about yoga." "He is a deal killer." "I can't work with her. She's such a drama queen." No one is that simple, that consistently flawed.

When we interact with our judgments rather than the whole, complex person, we choke off any possibility of creative, positive communication, as well as the opportunity to learn.

The trick to avoiding misuse of your belief system is to understand how it works, and when to shut it off. When you encounter another person (or object or situation), your fear of not-knowing

The Power to Control Judgment

kicks in. You quickly scan your memories for recognition so that you can apply the appropriate label and categorize the individual without taking the time and effort to get to know him or her. "Ah, a HOMELESS PERSON: lazy, dirty, stinky, drug and alcohol addicted, mentally ill, probably dangerous." Move to the other side of the street.

> As soon as the label is applied, the labeler can relax—stress relieved, crisis averted. Security restored.
> That's how it feels anyway.

Unfortunately, this process, which maintains our false sense of control over the universe, diminishes both the labeled and the labeler. The harm to the **labeled** is most obvious. They feel discounted, unseen, unheard and misjudged. The "homeless person" could be an astrophysicist who became overwhelmed with her responsibilities and just decided to drop out for a while—who knows? **Labelers** harm themselves by missing the opportunity to get to see the individual, to learn and expand their understanding of the world—perhaps even learn a little astrophysics. Maybe make a new friend.

Even though I have spent years teaching others about the lost opportunities and dangers of judgment, I recently noticed that I could use a refresher course. Like with my road rage experiment, slips happen. I realized that I was uncomfortable and intimidated by two guys who work out at the gym I frequent. One was a Latino boxer—big, tough-looking fellow who always seemed so intense—never seemed to smile. I had never spoken to him but had him labeled as an angry, aggressive and probably dangerous person. The other was even more mysterious—a big guy with long, unruly black hair who wore unlaced combat boots rather than athletic shoes. No one ever spoke to him. It seemed like everyone in the gym was intimidated by or frightened of these guys.

I developed a growing discomfort with my apparent judgments of these two men. I didn't know them, yet I'd decided that they were scary people—avoid. These thoughts were incongruent with my belief that I am a loving, accepting, inclusive person. Something had to give: I decided I had to get to know them. I gave myself two weeks to engage each of them in conversation. When I did, the two guys got me out in the alley and beat the crap out of me. NO—just kidding. To my surprise, shame and utter delight, I found both men to be sweet, lovely people. What an eye opener. If you haven't done this in a while, give it a try.

There are few things in this world more gratifying than exposing and exploding a prejudice.

In workshops, I often refer to reliance on stored prejudgments as "autopilot." When you see an intimidating dog, off leash, it is helpful to allow your autopilot to guide you to the other side of the street. To prevent misuse of this tool, you need to be aware when to use it and when to turn it off. When you encounter an angry Eskimo, you have the ability (once you liberate this SuperPower) to shut off autopilot and thoughtfully examine the situation. "Okay, I had a bad encounter with an Eskimo—that doesn't mean that all Eskimos are dangerous and potentially violent." You may choose to engage him or her in conversation, then see how you feel about this individual Eskimo.

> **When you engage rather than judge, you penetrate beneath the simple labels to reveal the complexity and beauty of the individual.**

Here is another example of the thoughtful use of your belief system in making small, day-to-day decisions. I am a condiment man. I love mayo. I can put mayo on just about anything short of Cheerios (and I'm thinking of trying that). Shopping on autopilot, I will buy a name-brand mayo made with olive oil. Why? Because I had prior experiences that led to stored beliefs like "I don't trust private brands" and "Too much fat in my diet is bad for my health; olive oil is safe."

If I were to turn off autopilot, my shopping experience might go like this: I research medical sites about the effects of various oils on the body. I discover that canola oil is also a healthy oil. I read the ingredients of brand-name and off-brand mayos and compare. I see that one of the off-brand mayos has canola oil, compare the ingredients to a name brand and discover that they are nearly identical. The off-brand mayo is $2 less than the name brand. I buy it instead. When you reject what you think you know, your senses open to the reality and complexity of the individual or situation. No two of us are alike, and everyone has something to teach if you're open to learning.

Criticism: What about when others judge you?

Judgment works both ways. You judge others and are judged by others (seems only fair)—in the form of criticism. Criticism is one person's attempt to protect their view of the world by negating yours. Just as you have an idyllic view of the world stored in your belief system, so does every other human on the planet. And every artificially created internal world-view is as unique as each person's complex variety of experiences.

Criticism feels like an attack, like you are being negated, diminished. But what feels like an attack is merely the other person protecting their sense of security. One or more of your beliefs differs from theirs, and they feel compelled to defend their "known universe." And the more fear-based and insecure the individual, the more critical they are of others.

Once you understand that the other person is just comparing their internal beliefs to yours, and feeling threatened, there is no need to counterattack. You can approach the other person with curiosity and compassion: "This issue is obviously important to you. We appear to disagree, but I would love to understand your point of view if you wouldn't mind." This response will yield more fruitful results than "Bite me, stupid wanker!"

Criticism and Praise: Which is Correct?

So that you don't read ahead, I'll tell you now. The answer is—NEITHER.

There is a university study that I find amusing. It attempts to answer the question: Which is more effective in improving leadership team performance: using positive feedback to let people know when they're doing well, or negative feedback, letting them know when they're off track? Their conclusions: "The average ratio for the highest-performing teams was 5.6 positive comments for every negative one. The medium-performance teams averaged 1.9 positive to 1 negative. But the average for the low-performing teams was only 0.36 to 1, or almost three negative comments for every positive one."

Praise feels terrific, but can be a trap. Even though there is no question that most of us are affected by positive and negative comments, you should understand that they are both about as useful as lips on a chicken. These comments, positive or negative, do not necessarily reflect who we are or the effectiveness of our actions. They are merely the result of the commenter comparing our actions or opinions to their stored beliefs. If our efforts support their views, they praise us. If they do not, they criticize. If you believe the praise, you are as likely to accept the criticism. This can be a problem when you consider that many humans criticize more than they praise. As Wayne Dyer says:

"If someone tells you how wonderful you are, you can treat that the same as if they tell you how awful you are."

In either case, the most you will gain, by analyzing their response, is a window into who *they* are.

What, me worry? Worry is judgment projected into the future.

From 1999 to 2009, I managed a high-profile, multi-office real estate company in Marin County. When I joined, they were a small entrepreneurial group owned by a local development firm. The owners were bright, creative and fun. The company was purchased six months later, by a large multinational corporation. Nine years later, that company sold to a financial conglomerate headquartered in Canada, which decided to sell our little operation off to the highest bidder. As a county manager, I had a high salary relative to other office managers in the area.

If you've ever been through a corporate sale or merger, you know that, in preparation for putting the company on the market, steps are taken to improve the profit and loss statement as quickly as possible—increasing the value on paper. The only way to affect the bottom line immediately is to reduce expenses. I knew I was a goner. My wife and I used to joke about whether I should stash some cardboard boxes in my trunk for all my stuff.

Sure enough, I got the boot. That night and the next morning, I was racked with worry. How would I pay the mortgage, provide for my family, send my girls to college, buy myself an 80-inch 4K Ultra HD TV, a European espresso machine? OMG, can you imagine my dread? What prospects would a fired, middle-aged manager have in a technology-fixated world that embraces youth?

Fearing a loss of security, I anticipated the worst—a total loss of income, divorce, bankruptcy. I even saw a cardboard box under a bridge in my future.

Somewhat surprisingly, within two days I was hired by an even bigger, more successful competitor who offered to open six real estate offices in Marin that I would manage. Within a week, 80 of the agents from the former firm followed me to the new company, and we were up and running—profitable from year one. This was one of many situations where I worried about future problems that never came to pass. This is not a new phenomenon. Five hundred years ago, Michel de Montaigne said:

"My life has been filled with terrible misfortune, most of which never happened." *Yes, I know Mark Twain said it too, just a few hundred years later.*

Modern studies show that 85 percent of what subjects worry about will never happen, and with the 15 percent that will occur, 79 percent will turn out better than expected or the unwanted result may teach them a lesson worth learning. This means that 97 percent of what you worry about is smoke.

The Power to Control Judgment

So, what's wrong with a little worry? Everybody does it, right? Right: Most people do worry, incessantly in fact, but there is plenty wrong with it. As a sales trainer and manager, I have observed the deleterious effects of worry, well beyond the mere wasting of time and energy.

Sales trainers will often separate time into four categories:
"A" time is time spent face-to-face with clients.
"B" time is completing activities that will result in "A" time.
"C" time is productive activities that are necessary to the job but do not lead directly to "A" time.
"D" time is time for yourself—time to study, exercise, relax.

What other trainers fail to mention is "W" time—probably because I made it up. This is time wasted on worry, self-recrimination, second-guessing and doubt. The big problem with "W" time is that it can intrude on all other times. "A" time can become "A/W" time, "B" time, "B/W" time, and so forth. Here is what "A/W" time looks like for a salesperson: You've clocked a lot of productive "B" time—calling clients, sending notes, knocking on doors, and you are about to meet with a new prospective buyer. Five minutes before your appointment you get a call from an agent on an unrelated transaction—she tells you that her buyer, the buyer of your listing, is asking for a $50,000 credit for termite work, terms you are sure your seller will never accept. You begin to think about how you will present the bad news to your seller. You imagine her yelling into the phone, blaming you for not being firm enough with the buyer's agent, threatening to cancel the sale and the listing. Your new prospects walk into your office.

You know the importance of this meeting. This is your moment to impress these prospects with your energy, your commitment, your knowledge, skill and experience. In other words, you need to be on your "A" game. If you are actually on your "A/W" game, worrying about the $50,000 credit request, you may think you're doing a good job—saying the right things. But if your mouth is saying one thing and your eyes and body language are saying something else, like "I'm a dead man," they will know it. They'll sense that you are not focused on them—intuit your lack of presence. Kiss that relationship goodbye.

Worry is a habit. Easy to live with when you're young—you think you have all the time in the world. Unfortunately, "W" time intrusions don't go away with age. Here is a quick suggestion for those who would like to reduce the worry habit:

Awareness. Notice when you worry. Say to yourself, "Here I go again," and focus on the present.

Embrace reality. It is not the perfect world you fantasize about where every dream comes true: you always get the job you want, your mom's attention, the biggest slice of apple pie. As I often tell my students, this isn't Disneyland. The boat you are navigating along the river of life is not running on a steel track. In the real world, S**T HAPPENS! As Dr. Richard Carlson says: "Life is rarely the way we would like it to be—it simply is. The greater our surrender to the truth of the moment, the greater our peace of mind." And remember, when we fight or reject reality, we forfeit the opportunity to learn from the real moment—increase our knowledge, skill and understanding. In addition to the effects worry has on behavior, there are health reasons for learning to be more serene.

Carolyn Gregoire, Senior Health & Science Writer at The Huffington Post, wrote: "The hormones stress and worry dump into your system shrinks brain mass, lowers your IQ, makes you prone to heart disease, cancer and premature aging, can predict marital problems, family dysfunction and depression, and makes seniors more likely to develop dementia and Alzheimer's." Now that has me worried!

Take the worry quiz

When you notice yourself worrying, take this little quiz:
1. Describe in detail the terrible thing you think is going to happen. What is the evidence that it will happen? What is the likelihood that it will occur?
2. What alternative (positive) outcomes are as likely or more likely to occur than your worry scenario?
3. What is the evidence that one or more of these more positive outcomes will occur? What is the likelihood?
4. If your worry scenario does occur, what is the worst that can happen? How would it affect you?
5. If your worry scenario does occur, will you accept it? If not, what will you do to shift the situation back to your desired outcome? How will you regroup and move forward? Having a plan in place to respond can reduce anxiety over the worry scenario.

In addition to these questions, it can be helpful to discuss your concerns with someone you trust. Perhaps they will bring a fresh perspective to the problem.

Even though your worry scenario is statistically unlikely to occur, if it does, don't resist. Resistance siphons creativity. Rather than addressing the event, you address your resistance. When the actual result fails to match your desired result, try taking the following steps:

1. Focus on the event, not your feelings. Accept that the worry scenario did unfold: It is now a current reality. Let go of your resentment and anger, your need to be right. You have nothing to defend: No one is right all the time. Remember, Edison invented 1,000 nonfunctional light bulbs before finally getting it right.
2. Examine this unwanted result. What is wrong with it? What is right with it? Does it solve any of the underlying problems?
3. If the actual result is still not acceptable, what can you do to improve it? With whom could you speak? What actions could you take?
4. Is there a compromise solution between your ideal scenario and the actual result? Seek out a proponent of the actual result. Listen openly to their arguments. You may decide that the actual result is worth trying. If you are still not convinced, discuss with them the possibilities of a compromise solution.
5. If you are in a long-term stressful situation, remember to exercise regularly, eat well and get plenty of sleep. Your general health can affect your anxiety level.
6. Take a few minutes each day to relax your mind. Ask for a solution to your problem and clear your mind. Write down any insights you may have. And remember to implement your good ideas: Thought without action is mental masturbation.

The Power to Control Judgment

It's clear that judging can create a world of problems for you and those around you. Ask yourself: Are you satisfied seeing the world through the filter of your stored beliefs, or would you like to, at least on occasion, look beyond your limited expectations at the raw, gritty, rich world *in which you actually live?* Are you willing to reject the false security of knowing and experience the unknown? If so, how do you see beyond the labels, beyond your stored beliefs, into the true nature of a person or situation?

For me, it is a matter of becoming aware of my worry-thoughts. On a hike, I can walk past beautiful natural landscapes without ever seeing them because I'm in my head, thinking about a problem, worrying about an outcome (this is especially scary when you're driving). Suddenly I look at where I am and realize that I don't remember how I got there. My body took me along my usual trail, but my mind was AWOL. I stop and look out into the trees, quiet my mind and soak in the view with new eyes. I don't blame myself for missing all the beauty while worrying about crap. I don't try to wrap up the thought, decide how to handle it later. I stop—turn off the thought machine and observe the present moment. This moment is what Eckhart Tolle calls "no-mind," a state of inner peace and stillness. When I do this in nature, I am no longer alone. I experience a sense of oneness with everything around me. (No, I don't hug trees. Tried it once but it was covered in ants and poison oak—wasn't pretty.) With practice, this inner peace of no-mind deepens and expands. And don't worry—being present is not like turning into a zombie. You become more alert, more awake and receptive than when you are in your head trying to force reality into the mold created by your stored beliefs.

TO FORGIVE WITHOUT JUDGMENT

Without judgment, you can forgive with compassion and understanding instead of first making the other person wrong.

We tend to think of forgiveness as a magnanimous act of kindness: "Look at what a good person I am. I forgive you." Puke. Forgiveness is self-serving and potentially disingenuous when coupled with judgment. Would we feel the need to forgive if we had not already judged the person wrong? That judgment, of course, comes from comparing the person's actions to our expectations. If they do not match up, we incline to make them wrong—so we can, of course, be right.

Forgiveness with judgment happens when you compare another's actions or beliefs to your own and judge them as being wrong. Then, even though you think them wrong, you magnanimously forgive them.

You love your dog and are surprised when a friend you've invited for dinner asks if you could put your dog in the bedroom. You are unaware of the fact that your friend was nearly killed in a dog attack when he was young. You comply with his wishes, but it eats at you for days, changes how you feel about this person whom you otherwise like very much. You just "know" that anyone who wants to lock away your sweet dog in the bedroom must be a dog hater. Finally, however, you decide that the friendship is more important so, even though he's a dirty dog hater, you magnanimously forgive him.

The Power to Control Judgment

"Learning to forgive without judgment requires that you transcend your ego's need to be right and make someone else wrong. In releasing judgment, you free yourself from the energy of resentment, betrayal, anger and hatred, and create space to live the love you deserve."
—*Carolyn Hidalgo, Coaches Training Institute*

When you cut the judgment out of the equation, you forgive because you understand that everyone is different. We have each had a unique series of experiences since conception that have molded our beliefs and, therefore, our behavior. We are all different—unique. So, who are we to forgive someone for being different than us?

The Judgment Mirror

Ending judgment is a worthy goal. Noticing your inclination to judge, however, can be a mirror into the world of self-judgment.

When you judge yourself for your beliefs or actions, you also judge others who express those same beliefs or actions. Why do this? Because your self-image wants to "be right." By projecting your unwelcome feelings onto others, you can express your indignation over their actions while maintaining a positive opinion of yourself, avoiding a loss of security by being wrong. Sneaky, aren't we?

There is, however, a silver lining to judging others. If you sharpen your awareness to where you quickly understand that your judgment of others is a mirror, you can obtain valuable insight into your self-concept. This is a great tool, helping you to see how you feel about *you*. You can then use these insights to forgive yourself.

If you notice the inclination to judge someone for being overly dramatic, say to yourself, "I forgive myself for every time I've made a bigger deal out of something than I needed to." If you want to judge someone for procrastinating, say to yourself, "I forgive myself for every time I have postponed a commitment or promise."

I used this technique while working to end my road rage when someone failed to look in their rear-view mirror and cut me off. Rather than judging that driver as an inept slob who should lose his license and give me his car, I would say to myself: "I forgive myself for my expectation to show up perfectly all of the time, and for all of the times that I haven't."

Health Benefits of Forgiveness

Holding onto anger and resentment can cause stress with all of its potential health hazards. Notes Karen Swartz, M.D., practicing psychiatrist and clinical programs director of the Johns Hopkins Mood Disorders Center: "If someone is stuck in an angry state, what they're essentially doing is being in a state of adrenaline. And some of the negative health consequences of not forgiving are high blood pressure, anxiety, depression, not having a good immune response."

Forgiveness *with* judgment also carries these potential health risks. If you can let go of your judgment and forgive from a state of compassion, you experience a release of tension. If, however, you profess forgiveness while holding on to anger and resentment, the pressure remains and may even increase.

Fred Luskin, Ph.D., director of the Stanford University Forgiveness Project, says, "Forgiveness boils down to a simple choice: whether to dwell over past hurts or try to see the good in others." He asks us to consider our intention: to dwell on what went wrong or, instead, see the goodness behind every act given you.

In the end, it is better to understand than to forgive—know that the other person is only being themselves and, in this instance, in conflict with your beliefs. That doesn't make them wrong, and it doesn't make them right. It makes them who they are. If they are projecting their self-judgments onto you, feel compassion for their pain. If there is nothing to judge, there is nothing to forgive.

SUPERPOWER SUMMARY

> The SuperPower here, should you choose to liberate it, is control over the filters of your stored belief system. Learn when to rely with autopilot and when to shut it off. When you replace knowing with sincere curiosity you see the real, complex person, not the judgment.
>
> And, when you are judged, no need to attack. Remember that the judge is simply doing what we have all done on many occasions—comparing your actions to their inner set of rules and finding a mismatch.
>
> If you stop judging, you will never have to forgive with judgment (which is more self-aggrandizing than an act of forgiveness). Then you can forgive the other with compassion, understanding that because their actions do not match your personal view of the world does not make them wrong. Forgive because you understand that everyone is different.

CHAPTER 5

POWERFULLY BAD WORDS

SUPERPOWER:
Stop judging your results as Successes or Failures.

There are 171,476 words in current use in the English language, according to the Second Edition of the 20-volume *Oxford English Dictionary*. The number varies of course, since we are continually adding new words while others pass into distant memory. Still others remain with altered meanings, such as:

Tweet: Used to be a sound made by happy birds. Now it is a post made on the social-media application Twitter.

Feed: Used to refer to the act of giving someone food. Now it is a place where everyone you've ever met posts pictures of their lunches, their babies, their hair and their engagement rings.

Bump: Used to be something you avoided to prevent your car from going out of alignment. Also referred to the first part of a dance move—the Bump and Grind. Now it refers to moving an online post or thread to the top of the reverse chronological list by adding a new comment or post to the thread.

Unplugged: Used to be how musicians re-recorded kick-ass rock songs on acoustic instruments to double the income from well-written tunes (example: Neil Sedaka's *Breaking Up is Hard to Do*). Now it means to refrain from using digital or electronic devices for a period.

I was surprised to learn that the also contains 47,156 obsolete words. See if you can guess the meaning of these old, out-of-use words. I'll even make it multiple choice. And, remember, these are not foreign-language words. They are, or were, in the: *Oxford English Dictionary*.

Mizzle-Kyted:
1. Lying on the belly
2. That has a red and blotchy belly
3. Having one's legs turn red and blotchy from sitting too near a fire

Quagswagging:
1. Resembling or characteristic of a duck
2. To chatter, babble, talk idly or senselessly
3. The action of shaking to and fro

Forplaint:
1. Covered in hair; hairy
2. Bad-tempered
3. Wearied and complaining

Sammyfoozle:
1. To intoxicate, make drunk, confuse, muddle
2. To make money in any way possible
3. To make a fool of; to cheat, con

Wanweird:
1. Slightly sad
2. Hard lot, ill fate, misfortune
3. Lasciviousness, lust

Is this fun or what? I wanted to include all 47,156 words, but my publishers wanted to keep the book under 2,000 pages—so cheap. The answers in order are 1, 3, 3, 3, 2.

Is there a point here? Yes. A little known (because I just made it up) way of categorizing words is those that were created in and whose meaning refers to real-world phenomenon, and those that were created in and whose meaning refers to CZ-World (short for Comfort Zone-world) phenomena.

Real-world words are easy to spot. They refer to a place or thing that EXISTS, like trees, rocks, root beer, Illinois (which I've never seen but assume exists), poker chips, sneezes, etc.

The ego fabricates CZ-world words. Examples of CZ-world words would be stress, fear, overwhelm, disastrous, sadness, happiness, satisfaction, jealousy—labels we give to feelings and events in our lives. These things do not exist in the real world. You can't see them, touch them or experience them except by choice. Stress, for instance, does not exist in the known universe. It is a chosen reaction to real or perceived actions. "Wait a minute," some of you are thinking, "I don't choose stress. I hate stress. Why would I choose stress, you awareness-freak wanker?"

At the moment, it may not seem like you choose to feel stress. That's because it isn't a considered response: "Geez that sucked. I think I'll feel a boatload of stress for a week, maybe two." No, it is an automatic response, a preselected reaction to real-world results that conflict with the unrealistic, ideal world you have created within your comfort zone. If you choose to be a slave to your internal image of life, you will most likely respond to conflicts with stress. When you learn to control the use of your "rule book," rather than letting it control you, you can accept unexpected or unwanted results with curiosity and learn from the experience—avoiding stress.

One way to differentiate between real-world and CZ-world words is that real-world words describe universal or shared objects. I sit and rest on a large red rock. If I walk away and you come along the same path, the rock you sit on is the same rock, although you may experience it somewhat differently. I may have thought it was comfortable while it hurts your boney butt. Despite different perceptions, it is still the same rock. CZ-world words are, in general, more experiential and not at all universal. For instance, the mortgage payment is due. I have not yet received any royalties on this book (GRRRR) and feel stress over my inability to pay the mortgage. You, in the same circumstance, may not feel stress at all due to your faith in your ability to generate money when needed.

The reason for all this word talk is that there are two often-used words which, in my opinion, should be moved to the obsolete section of the dictionary. They are CZ-world words that do not describe anything that exists in the universe. These words are:

FAILURE and SUCCESS

Like most CZ-world words, failure and success do not live in the world and are not universally experienced. They are words we use to label real-world events, but they are not the events. They are judgments made by the user and by observers. Here is a real-life example with me as the user:

After selling real estate for four years, I decided it was time to manage an office. After all, I had a management degree, was the top salesman in my office and liked bossing people around—kidding. I had discovered and fostered some helpful SuperPowers like training, coaching and communication skills. Right around this time, my office manager, Dick, announced that he was retiring. I went to the owner of the company and asked to be Dick's replacement. The other agents in the office signed a petition requesting me for the job. The owner, however, thought that I was too young. He wanted me to get a few more years of experience. Not one to be deterred by the good opinions of others, I decided to open and manage a brokerage—along with two partners. Even with three of us, we were not well funded: I think we had about $15,000 to invest—not much for a startup operation. So, we got creative. We bought used medal desks from an office closure in San Francisco, had Formica tops prefabbed and painted them ourselves. To decorate the walls, we found material we liked at a fabric store and constructed a series of tapestries. We located two blocks from our old office, which helped us to recruit most of the agents from our old employer. It was a blast. The owner of my former office was a real gentleman about it, by the way, and later even hired me to manage one of his offices.

Unfortunately, we only had six months of the excellent market before a nasty recession. When interest rates got up around 20 percent, the real estate market came to a grinding halt. I was managing 20 people at the time so I was not creating any income from sales and, since we were not yet profitable, not taking a salary. I spent most of my time talking my agents out of depression or a decision to leave the business. A year or so into the recession, my partners and I began pumping our personal funds into the company, hoping that we could keep it afloat until the economy improved. At the time, I owned a lovely home and a rental condo, and my second wife had just given birth to our first daughter, Moorea.

First to go was the condo, then the house, then the balance on all of our credit cards. I thought of selling Moorea to a Saudi prince, but my wife wouldn't hear of it (Just kidding, Moorea).

After nearly two years, the recession was still hanging on, but I wasn't. I was broke, owned no real estate, had $80,000 in credit card debt, turned in our rental cars and bought a used Fiat with a frozen driver's door. My partners and I got out of our lease and rented a much smaller location that only accommodated two of our agents and us. Everyone else moved to larger, better-funded brokerages. I needed a job. It was hard to abandon the business but harder to ask my wife to stretch that lone chicken breast into a third dinner for three.

I felt awful.

I was a failure, utterly humiliated, doubting that I would ever get another job in real estate management.

Why would anyone hire a guy who just failed so miserably? I was resigned to the fact that I would either return to sales—not a great prospect given the tenacity of the recession—or get a paying job. I had worked construction in the past, drove a delivery truck. I'd find something.

To my amazement, I began receiving management offers as soon as the word of my "failure" got around the industry. I didn't get it at first. Were they crazy? Turns out that starting the business the way I did, as the youngest broker in Marin County, had earned the respect of the industry, despite everything that had transpired. Within two years our debts were paid off, and we were able to purchase another home. This is the message, the lesson I learned, and have learned over and over throughout my life:

Judging any life event as good or bad is folly.

We never know what opportunities an apparent failure may lead to, or how fast an evident success can fade. The day I quit my brokerage business, I was sure that this was just about the worst day of my life. I was friggin' depressed. It turned out that losing that business was the start of a long and very successful management career.

Years later I was working as the county manager for a large Bay Area firm, managing about 160 agents. It was the first year of another recession and, as mentioned previously, the multinational firm that owned the company decided to sell. Once again, I found myself out of work.

My apparent "failure" quickly turned into an even better opportunity, demonstrating once again the folly of judging any experience as either good or bad, success or failure. So, no harm, right? Everything worked out.

I'd say I was very fortunate to realize the folly of my judgments so quickly. It doesn't always work out that well. What if my phone had been silent for a few weeks? Judging an event as a failure can be dangerous. A person who judges things as bad can become moody, depressed. Their sadness over the closing door can blind them to the one that just opened. Their depressed mood can lead to lost opportunities, lost friends—and can lead to self-destructive behavior, even suicide.

Failure is nothing more than a label we place on unexpected, unwanted outcomes. If we drop the label and view every result with curiosity, as an opportunity to learn and grow, risk becomes a way of life.

We then discover that the most significant risk in life is *not* taking risks.

Eventually, we see that there are no risks, only results. We only perceive an act, or outcome, as risky because it is outside of our beliefs, our comfort zone. When a reporter asked Edison, "How did it feel to fail one-thousand times?" Edison replied, "I didn't fail one-thousand times. The light bulb was an invention with one-thousand steps."

I could go on and on with examples of how prematurely judging a situation as good or bad is usually wrong. And I'm sure that you can come up with your examples.

Living the good life, one filled with joy, love and abundance (that's my definition of the good life), is made more difficult if we are derailed by our judgments—especially when it comes to success or failure.

Simply stated, life is. Shakespeare wrote in Hamlet, Act 2, Scene 2: **"...there is nothing either good or bad but thinking makes it so."**

I'm always fascinated to hear that some of what I assume are modern, New Age ideas have been around for decades, centuries or, in some cases, millennia. This from Virgil, a Roman poet (70 BCE-19 BCE) born in the Andes near Mantua, Italy:

"Perhaps someday it will be pleasant to remember even this."

Years before the Common Era, before Christ, Virgil was acknowledging that even an event that seemed terrible indeed might be considered pleasant in time.

There is an ancient Sufi story from the days of Lao Tzu in China that demonstrates the folly of judgment. This version is a translation by Paulo Coelho, a Brazilian lyricist and novelist who in early 2017 was nominated by the Albert Einstein Foundation as one of the 100 leading visionaries of our time:

Many years ago, in a poor Chinese village, there lived a farmer and his son. His only material possession, apart from the land and a small hut, was a horse he had inherited from his father.

One day, the horse ran away, leaving the man with no animal with which to work the land. His neighbors, who respected him for his honesty and diligence, went to his house to say how much they regretted his loss. He thanked them for their visit but asked:

'How do you know that what happened was a misfortune in my life?'

Someone muttered to a friend: 'He obviously doesn't want to face facts, but let him think what he likes; after all, it's better than being sad about it.'

And the neighbors went away again, pretending to agree with what he had said.

A week later, the horse returned to its stable, but it was not alone; it brought with it a beautiful mare for company. The inhabitants of the village were thrilled when they heard the news, for only then did they understand the reply the man had given them, and they went back to the farmer's house to congratulate him on his good fortune.

'Instead of one horse, you've got two. Congratulations!' they said. 'Many thanks for your visit and your solidarity,' replied the farmer. 'But how do you know that what happened was a blessing in my life?'

The neighbors were rather put out and decided that the man must be going mad, and, as they left, they said: 'Doesn't the man realize that the horse is a gift from God?'

A month later, the farmer's son decided to break the mare in. However, the animal bucked wildly and threw the boy off;

the boy fell awkwardly and broke his leg so could not help with the harvest.

The neighbors returned to the farmer's house, bringing presents for the injured boy. The mayor of the village solemnly presented his condolences to the father, saying how sad they all were about what had occurred.

The man thanked them for their visit and their kindness, but he asked: 'How do you know that what happened was a misfortune in my life?' These words left everyone dumbstruck because they were all quite sure that the son's accident was a real tragedy. As they left the farmer's house, they said to each other: 'Now he really has gone mad; his only son could be left permanently crippled, and he's not sure whether the accident was a misfortune or not!'

A few months went by, and Japan declared war on China. The emperor's emissaries scoured the country for healthy young men to be sent to the front. When they reached the village, they recruited all the young men, except the farmer's son, whose leg had not yet mended.

None of the young men came back alive. The son recovered, and the two horses produced foals that were all sold for a good price. The farmer went to visit his neighbors to console and to help them since they had always shown him such solidarity. Whenever any of them complained, the farmer would say: 'How do you know that what happened was a misfortune?' If someone were overjoyed about something, he would ask: 'How do you know that what happened was a blessing?' And the people of the village came to understand that life has other meanings that go beyond mere appearance. — Traditional Sufi story, January 30, 2008, by Paulo Coelho, paulocoelhoblog.com.

Judgments may also be revealed as Bantha Poodoo when viewed from a different time, different perspective, another place or when we are in a different mood. Not very reliable, are they? Zorba the Greek described himself as "the whole catastrophe." He celebrated the reality of who he was—accepting rather than judging himself.

One of the SuperPowers I hope you are willing to liberate and ignite is your ability to accept the world as it is—not expect it to conform to the unrealistic, false world you've created within.

Our actions affect the world around us. While we cannot expect to manifest all our dreams precisely as imagined, we can nudge the world in our chosen direction. For me, that is enough. I've come to accept that I am not alone on the planet, that my desires are only one spoke in the wheel of life. And, for me, that is just fine, because it is the truth, it is a reality. And I'd much rather live within a potentially gnarly REAL world than struggle to manipulate what *is* in my fantasy about how it should be.

We are not living in a Disneyland ride where boats are on tracks, animals are programmed machines and life is perfect so long as you have a multi-day, park-hopper ticket with early admission to Magic Morning. We are soft, vulnerable creatures living on a giant, often inhospitable rock with a molten interior and shifting land masses, spinning along the equator at roughly 1,000 mph while hurling around the sun at nearly 67,000 mph, while our solar system is swirling around the galaxy at about 490,000 mph. What could go wrong?

Life can be messy; so what? "Life is a daring adventure or nothing," Helen Keller observed. You could say it isn't perfect, but that is only in comparison to your false construct within. It is perfect—has to be—because it is. Every morning, when I write gratitude statements, I start by giving thanks for another day on our "Chaotically Perfect World." It is what we have, where we live. Don't judge it; embrace it.

SUPERPOWER SUMMARY

> The key to unlocking this SuperPower is to stop judging your results as Successes or Failures. If you think about it, it is unlikely that your goals, dreams, wishes and visions will always manifest exactly as you see them in your mind's eye. Perhaps if you were the only person on earth you could get pretty close, but you aren't. For every goal you have, there are untold numbers of people with the same goal and untold numbers with conflicting goals, and everything in between. The result of all the forces and intentions being leveled at a given situation will depend on the mix of intentions, the energy each person invests in their desired outcome, plus environmental conditions, overall societal pressures and many other contributing forces.
>
> Am I saying that you shouldn't even bother having goals? Not at all. You just need to adjust your expectations or be ready for a lot of disappointment. Accept results as the new reality, then decide whether to move on or continue taking actions to effect change.

CHAPTER 6

THE POWER OF ACCEPTANCE— RESISTANCE IS FUTILE

SUPERPOWER:
Stop resisting what is. Accept what has already occurred and respond to the event rather than to your opposition to the event.

Events may create physical pain, but they do not in themselves create suffering. Resistance creates suffering. Stress happens when your mind resists what is. The only problem in your life is your mind's resistance to life as it unfolds."
— Dan Millman, *Way of the Peaceful Warrior*

You are limited in your capacity to achieve by the time and energy you spend resisting. How much more could you accomplish if you eliminated all the blocked energy caused by resistance? The relationship between resistance and acceptance is so vital to liberation that it deserves its own chapter.

The Power of Acceptance—Resistance is Futile

Why Resist What Has Already Happened?

It does sound kind of bonkers, doesn't it—resisting something that has already come to pass? We do it all the time—resist any outcome that conflicts with what we desire and expect. It gives us a false sense of security to believe that our version of the world is right and the one in front of our noses is wrong.

What's wrong with resisting? Don't be such a wimp!

For one thing, resistance is the primary path to stress. Not that stress is ever required. It is a reaction we have decided (on a subconscious level) is appropriate when we resist an actual result that's different from the one we wanted and anticipated.

Another problem with resistance is that it's a big waste of time. There were several recessions during the years that I managed real estate offices. Observing agent reactions to significant market changes was like a master course in change response. When sales volume slows down, most agents resist. Fearing a loss of income, they begin by denying the problem: "Recession my patootie. It's just a seasonal lull. I'm sure the market will bounce back next month." When that fails to happen, they spend precious time deciding who to blame: the government, the Federal Reserve, their company, China, their spouse, gluten…

When they run out of people willing to engage in conversations about whose fault it is, they are finally forced to concede the change. If they choose to keep working, they will analyze the new market and make appropriate changes to their business plan. But the fact that they've lost six months of business resisting the change will have a significant impact on their income.

At the same time, there are always a few agents who take

market transitions in stride. No denial. No blame. They see what's coming and alter their actions to take advantage of the new environment. When the most recent recession began, the luxury market in Marin County dived off a very steep cliff. The lower-end market, however, picked up dramatically, unfortunately due to the number of people who were losing their homes in foreclosure or short sale. One of my most successful luxury agents saw what was coming and quickly cut her promotional budget in luxury neighborhoods—instead promoting herself in lower-priced areas of the county. Not surprisingly, her business continued to flourish.

> **Events don't cause stress. Resistance to the event triggers a preprogrammed stress reaction.**

Even though it is the resistance to life that creates suffering, we tend to blame the event. I hear it all the time. People also get angry as if I am challenging their right to stress out: "Of course I'm stressed out! I just lost my job, my transmission and brakes both need to be replaced, and my daughter dyed her hair purple!"

Let's assume you have stored beliefs like, "They can't fire me, I'm too valuable," or "Cars should work perfectly—always—because I don't have the time or money to deal with major problems," or "My daughter is a good girl, she would never do anything stupid like those other kids." When your daughter calls you, panicked because she took your car to get her hair dyed purple and en route the transmission fell onto the road, resulting in you getting fired for missing an important meeting, you encounter reality in direct conflict with your expectations. Your secure world is threatened. You resist. The feeling you associate with resistance is stress. To reduce or eliminate the stress, you:

The Power of Acceptance—Resistance is Futile

1. **Deny reality.** "They won't fire me. They're just angry."
2. **Blame someone.** "Your mother told you it was okay to dye your hair purple, didn't she?"
3. **Fight reality.** Cut off your daughter's hair and ground her for two years, demand a new car since the one that broke down is apparently a lemon, and tell off your boss for being such a jerk.

Can you see any of these things working?

If you try to solve an event while resisting, you are not dealing with the facts; you are dealing with your resistance, trying to force the outcome into your preconceived image of how it should be. Your attempts to alter what has already occurred will almost always turn out bad. For one thing, you piss off a lot of people, like your daughter, boss and the car dealer.

Dealing with your resistance means dealing with your fears and desires—instead of dealing with the event. You compare the actual event with your preconceived image of how it should be. If they are too disparate, driven by fear of diminished security, your mind goes into full gear trying to manipulate reality so that it matches your image. If instead of defending your ego, you dealt with the situation, you could focus on the best outcome for all involved, including yourself.

In the Introduction, I mentioned the article I published so that I could create a speaking gig. That article was titled *White Knight Syndrome*. The hypothesis was that the primary reason for the loss of real estate sales transactions is not lousy pest reports or undisclosed defects—it is the agent's failure to maintain a detached, professional demeanor in the face of problems.

Problems arise when we compare reality to our expectations and find reality lacking. A real estate sales example:

A struggling agent lists a luxury home just in time to prevent her bankruptcy. It sells quickly, and her anxiety begins to ease. That is, until she gets a call from the buyer's agent asking for a $140,000 credit for work revealed by inspections. At this point, a good, professional agent will collect as much information as he or she can about the inspection reports and the buyer's motives, and perhaps even suggest that the sellers obtain their own work estimates. She will tell the buyer's agent that she will discuss the request with her sellers and get back to him.

The White Knight responds like this: "One-hundred-forty thousand?! Are you out of your effing mind! My sellers came way off their initial price! They have bent over backward for your greedy buyers. You go back and tell them that they are not getting another penny from us!!!!!"

Now, you'll notice that she has given a verbal counter offer to the buyer's agent without even informing the seller of the $140,000 request. Suppose the buyer gets angry when their agent recounts his phone call with the listing agent, back out and buy another home? Then the sellers tell their agent that it is such a shame the buyer didn't ask for a credit since they are so motivated they would probably have accepted. Oops!

By dealing with her resistance (out of fear of bankruptcy), the sellers' agent failed to deal with the actual event, violated her fiduciary duty to the client and, in the end, may have cost them a lot of time and money. Learning to let go of fears and insecurities and deal with events instead of resistance is what Richard Carlson described as "Lighting a candle instead of cursing the darkness."

The Cure for Resistance: Acceptance

Suffering is not created by having goals that guide your actions. Pain arises when we do not accept the results.

When you stop resisting, you transform the world from a problematic, stress-filled battleground into a beautiful, exciting, fun-filled joy ride.

For years I had difficulties with the idea of "acceptance." I thought it was total crap, a spineless, self-defeating excuse wimpy awareness freaks used to justify their passivity. I especially hated this ancient quote:

"The great way is not difficult for those who have no preferences."

To me, this quote from Hsin-Hsin Ming, The Third Patriarch of Zen, was analogous to "Don't ask for too much and you'll never be disappointed." It said to me that I should just lay back and take whatever horrors life throws my way. If I forget about goals or aspirations of any kind, life will be comfortable. Yeah, easy, if you don't mind wearing a loincloth and begging in the streets with a rice bowl. After years of struggling with this concept, I did finally get it—of course, this was after I became an insufferable awareness freak. Ha!

To have no preferences does not mean that we care for nothing. It means we care about everything. We embrace the endless variety of experiences the world has to offer. It means having faith that whatever the outcome, it will be okay. Acceptance is letting go of the reins, closing your eyes and trusting in the adventure.

Here's what I've learned acceptance does *not* mean:

- We should not fight for what we want.
- We should be okay with loss.
- We should roll over and accept it when we do not attain our goals.

Acceptance does not mean that you must allow every event or situation you encounter to merely happen no matter how wrong you believe it to be. Confused yet? I was. If you have ever attended an AA or Al-Anon meeting, you've heard "The Serenity Prayer," which is the common name for a prayer written by the American theologian Reinhold Niebuhr (1892–1971). This is as a good explanation for when to let go and when to push for change:

God, grant me the serenity to accept the things I cannot change,
Courage to change the things I can,
And wisdom to know the difference.

I think this is as good a guide as any for those seeking a healthy approach to change. If an event has already happened and you either can't change it or decide that it is as good or better than the outcome you had hoped for, then accept it and move on. If you believe there is a better outcome that you have a chance of facilitating, go for it.

When you accept an outcome, you are merely acknowledging how life works.

The Power of Acceptance—Resistance is Futile

You have always dreamed of opening a pizza parlor. You drive by the perfect vacant building for your business and see a "For Lease" sign in the window. This is it! Time to make your dream come true. You create a vision board with photos of pizzas, of people laughing and enjoying life with a slice in one hand and a brew in the other. You research everything you can about opening a small business in this industry. You do some self-analysis. Do you have the knowledge and skills necessary to open and run a successful pizza parlor? If not, you read books, take a class or two at the local community college, perhaps even go to work in a pizza joint to learn the trade from the ground up. You are so ready and so confident that you quit your high-paying job in the securities industry and begin taking actions to make your dream happen.

Because you'll need a use permit from the city, you prepare a detailed, thoughtful presentation for the planning commission meeting. To your dismay, the commission turns you down, based primarily on the testimony of several local merchants who show up to protest that pizza parlors promote juvenile delinquency with their video games and loud music, not to mention the health issues created by all that cheese, pepperoni, sausage and lard. The merchants want something more sophisticated in the location like another dress store—which would be #31 in the downtown area.

Just like that. Rejected after one meeting. Do you respond with resistance or acceptance?

Resistance Response: The contrast between the actual result—no pizza parlor—and your idea of an idyllic unfolding of your lifelong dream hits you like a ton of mozzarella. Your ego rails at this horrible injustice. You go home and tell your wife how you've been treated. She leaves you. Well, hey, you did leave a good job and failed to deliver on the promised replacement. You decide to have a bottle of rum for lunch, write a scathing editorial in the local paper about "scumbags" on the planning commission and get sued by the city. To prove the merchants wrong, after hurling dog-poop bombs onto all their storefronts, you open a pizza place in a ratty, rundown part of town where no use permit is required. You fill it with video games and a loud jukebox. The cops arrest you for promoting gang violence; you receive a 10-year sentence that gets extended to 15 because they find your fingerprints on the bags that held the dog poop.

Acceptance Response: You accept the conclusion of the planning commission, understanding that they were only responding to the wishes of many dissenting merchants. You hire a land use attorney and begin planning for your appeal to the city council. In the meantime, you schedule meetings with several of the merchants who spoke against your plan. You share with them research as to the positive community effects of pizza parlors, invite them to a taste testing, giving them a role in the selection of your menu and make concessions about the number and types of video games you'll provide and the style and volume of the music. No gangster rap allowed. You obtain a permit and open shop.

Reactivity vs. Responsiveness

When an unwanted outcome meets ego, ego resists and reacts in a preprogrammed manner based on stored beliefs. Rather than a calm contemplation of the result, we judge and react, with no consideration of whether the outcome is as good or better than the one we attempted to manifest. We interpret the result as a personal affront: it's not what we wanted at all. We feel insulted. We defend or retaliate.

In **reaction mode,** we make quick, ill-considered decisions, ones we are likely to regret. The ego's panicked need to make us right creates pressure: We feel stress in our bodies. And the person or people we are interacting with will likely feel annoyance, anger—potentially damaging relationships. As a bonus, in reactive mode, we fail to see opportunities, fail to grow. We are so focused on redeeming ourselves, proving that our original assessment of the situation was right, that we forget to respond to the actual event.

Responsive mode: When we become aware of pending reactivity, we can move our response from our ego/outer self to our inner self—that part of us that is calm, flexible and free of the limitations of our stored beliefs. We take nothing personally. Rather than judging based on prior experience, we open to divergent opinions. We ask questions, curious about the outcome and how well it may resolve the situation at hand. This measured, dispassionate response garners respect from others, facilitates collaboration, and will result in more effective outcomes.

"After a period of time transforming your state from reactive to responsive, responsiveness will become your default state—fertile ground for success." — *Richard Carlson*

SUPERPOWER SUMMARY

> The SuperPower you may wish to liberate here is to stop resisting what is. Accept what has already occurred and respond to the event instead of to your resistance of the event. Your life path is long, unpredictable and unlimited. You can insist that your journey follow, perfectly, the map you hold in your mind, and suffer each deviation. Or you can enjoy the journey and choose to embrace each bend in the road with curiosity and gratitude. The choice, as always, is yours.

CHAPTER 7

THE POWER OF UNCONITIONAL HAPPINESS

SUPERPOWER:
Detach happiness from achievement or any other condition. Make happiness a moment-by-moment choice.

"When most of us think about what makes us happy, we tend to focus on the things in life that we crave or long to possess. These things may be concrete consumables, or they may be intangible resources, such as time, inner peace or true love."
—Suzanne Degges-White, Ph.D., writing for *Psychology Today*

Listen to people speak of happiness and you will usually hear a discussion of what will "make me happy":

"If I could only afford a new car, I'd be happy."

"If I could lose 50 pounds, life would be awesome. I'd finally be happy."

"I won't be happy until I fully fund my retirement."

This thought-trap of needing "something" to be happy is demonstrated in this never-ending folk story. I don't know the origin—it may be oral history. This is my version and may vary (considerably) from the original text.

Boy, life's a drag now, but wait until I graduate and get a real job. Then I'll be happy.

Well, that job sucked. Maybe I'll try another career. Yeah, if I find the right job, then I'll be happy.

That job sucked too. Maybe it's work that sucks. Perhaps I need a relationship. If I can find a wife, preferably one with enough money so that I can stop working, then I'll be happy.

Wow, who knew marriage would be so much work. I know, a child! If we have a child, our relationship will be complete; then I'll be happy.

Was I crazy! Kids are hard as hell, messy, expensive and smelly—and it just made the marriage worse. I know. We need a house, a home for our expanding family. Then I'll be happy.

Jeez, the house isn't as nice as our old apartment. I know, we'll remodel. Then I'll be happy.

House looks great now, but who knew owning would cost so much. I know, if I can refinance at a reasonable rate, I'll be happy.

Refinance my ass! By the time everything was rolled in, and a ton of fees, we're paying a lot more than our old rent, and the place isn't as beautiful. I'll never be happy!

And on and on it goes.

Conditional happiness gives us a few brief moments of pleasure when a condition is met but never lasts. Kahlil Gibran voiced this sentiment in *The Eye of the Prophet*:

"Joy is a myth that we seek. And when we find joy, it angers us, just as the river which hastens towards the plain slows down and darkens when it arrives there. For men are only happy through their aspiration to the heights. And when they achieve their aim, they become disillusioned and aspire to other, longer journeys."

This is the folly of seeking joy through achievement. It is why so many artists and entertainers have ended their own lives, intentionally through suicide, or less intentionally through accidental overdose or some other form of excess. They attained the heights of their professions only to find disillusionment.

The end of the journey, even with the destination reached, deprives us of direction and purpose. It can seem like the only release from this despair is to set new goals, aspire to new heights. The result of that strategy is a driven life in which happiness is forever dependent upon success and the continuous existence of unattained goals. Don't get me wrong; it's fun to achieve. You just shouldn't ask more of your accomplishments than temporary delight, or your happiness will turn to despair.

Unhappiness is the result of your struggle against the natural flow of life. When you're experiencing pleasure, you want it to last forever—it never does. When you're experiencing pain, you want it to go away immediately—it usually does not, at least not as quickly as you'd like.

If you pursue a dream but fall short of achievement, you are disappointed. When you achieve a goal, you're elated for a short time. Once the temporary happiness fades, you seek another result. We, humans, are like happiness junkies needing new, better fixes to maintain the high. What do we do when we're sad? We run out and buy a quart of rum raisin gelato and watch the first Harry Potter movie for the 50th time—whatever brings us comfort.

This is a perfect treadmill—a hamster cage—continually pursuing experiences we hope will fulfill our expectations and "make me happy." SPOILER: this doesn't work! So why keep doing it—seeking more significant achievements, chasing pleasure like a fox in a henhouse, thinking it will bring happiness?

The answer to this apparent problem—how to get happiness if you can't pursue it—comes from this quote:

"There is no way to happiness. Happiness is the way."

I first read this message in Wayne Dyer's 1978 book, *Pulling Your Own Strings*, although it has been attributed to Buddha, Thich Nhat Hanh, A. J. Muste, and Robert Ferre, to name only a few.

Short as it is, I believe that if you're going to glue one quote onto your bathroom mirror and tattoo it to your forehead, this should be it. It suggests the shift from conditional happiness to happiness by choice. If, as a species, we understood these ten words (yeah, go ahead and count: it's 10), there would be little need for antidepressants. We would eat less "comfort food," make fewer impulse purchases, slash the divorce rate, reduce the demand for illegal drugs, and convert most of our prisons into condos or college dormitories. This is an important point, so let's emphasize it with a quote from famed psychologist, singer, songwriter and committed Rastafari Bob Marley:

"Love the life you live. Live the life you love."

Or, from the Dalai Lama, another very bright, spiritual guy:

"The purpose of life is to be happy."

Notice the Dalai Lama did not say "achieve" happiness. He didn't say, "seek" happiness, "find" happiness or "pursue" happiness. The purpose of life is to "*BE* happy." We are taught from birth that we must earn happiness. Even our Declaration of Independence tells us that one of our inherent and inalienable rights is the "pursuit of happiness."

You don't have to have a Ph.D. to recognize the training program: From infancy, we learn that if we act in specific ways, we make people happy. Act in other ways and they become sad or angry. A baby screams and her parents freak out. She stops; they smile and coo.

Happiness is not a reward. It is a choice. Nothing can make you happy, but you can carry happiness with you wherever you go.

That's not how we act, however. We are forever creating lists of what "will make me happy." If you don't believe me, go ahead, start a list of all the things you think will make you happy. No rush—I'll wait. Okay, got it? Now rip it up! Once and for all, release the fantasy that your life must change in one way or another for you to be blissfully happy.

Wayne Dyer taught that if you can't be happy with the life you've created up to now, you'll never be satisfied when you achieve a goal—because you've never learned to be happy in the present. You're always searching for some future moment you imagine will make you happy.

If you need things or circumstances to make you happy, you will be forever chasing the rainbow. Even when you catch it, you will desire a bigger, brighter rainbow with a larger pot of gold at its end, and then a pony and cotton candy… When you tether happiness to achievement, all you know is striving. Conditional happiness is not an imperative, however. You were not born with a conditional happiness gene.

> **Conditional Happiness is a habit. You have the power to change it.**

How do you break any habit? Practice. Practice. Practice. The first step, once you have identified an old pattern you wish to abandon and, perhaps, a new pattern to take its place is to focus on the new behavior. One way to coax your subconscious into focusing on a new behavior is through your gratitude practice. When I wanted to curtail my road anger (rage is too intense a term), I created affirmations like:

"I become calm and relaxed when road hazards appear."

"When another driver cuts me off in traffic, I stay calm, take defensive action and keep going."

"I understand that everyone has a bad day. Everyone makes mistakes."

Of course, the choice of words and phrases is entirely personal. The words you write will be ones that speak to you. Unfortunately, as we've acknowledged, goals regarding happiness almost always refer to it as a feeling you will experience *after achieving something*:

"If I can only make this sale today, the pressure will be off. Life will be good." As a goal this could be worded, "I am so happy that I made the sale at 123 Main Street and paid off all my debts."

"If I get this promotion, everything will be fine. I will finally be happy." As a goal: "I am thrilled and happy now that I was promoted to plant supervisor. Life is so good."

Do you see the problem with these? The problem is that both of these goal statements make happiness contingent. Make a sale = get happy. Get promoted = get happy. What if you don't make the sale or get the promotion? No happiness? What then: sadness, disappointment, depression? Sounds like a blast to me.

Instead of making happiness the result of achieving this or that, make happiness a goal—independent of all other goals. In my goal achievement workshop, we refer to happiness as the "Master Goal," because it is the root of every other goal.

I need you to retrieve the list of goals you just tore up and tape it back together. Notice what all these goals have in common. Right: They are all things that you believe will make you happy. Since you now know that nothing can "make you happy," beyond a flash of momentary delight, you can adjust your thinking to be consistent with the way the world works—and you can tear up the list again—and, this time, toss it in the fireplace.

"Learn to be happy with what you have, while you pursue all that you want."   — Jim Rohn

Don't get me wrong; I'm not suggesting that you stop setting goals. They engage your creativity and focus your attention on the information and resources around you that can assist you to achieve. But don't expect too much of your successes. Don't kid yourself into believing that they are pathways to happiness. Transitory pleasure, sure. No problem. I like pleasure. But, you know how your mind works—as soon as you achieve one goal, the next one arises. Goodbye happiness, hello striving. Stop looking for a path to happiness and recognize that you're there.

Happiness is a state of mind, a decision, a choice; not a path.

Set a goal that you will own a particular car by a specific date—because you want the car, not because you hope it will "make you happy." Then, remember to set a goal that you remain a happy person regardless of the circumstance. The following are some sample happiness affirmations to get you started:

"Today I will be happy and content no matter what happens."

"My happiness makes all the people around me happy, expanding my happiness out into the world."

"I am happy, every day in every way."

"My happy disposition attracts more happiness into my life. People are attracted to me because of my infectious smile."

"I am happy with my life exactly as it is. Life is great."

"Being happy comes easily to me. It is my natural state of being."

"My happiness is unconditional. Whatever happens, I accept what I can't change, and will seek to change the things I can. No matter the outcome, I am happy."

"For me, happiness is my constant companion, no matter what is going on in my life."

"I am kind; I am loving; I am happy."

We'll end with a quote from that great American philosopher, Groucho Marx:

"I, not events, have the power to make me happy or unhappy today. I can choose which it shall be. Yesterday is dead; tomorrow hasn't arrived yet. I have just one day, today, and I'm going to be happy in it."

SUPERPOWER SUMMARY

> The SuperPower offered here is to make happiness a choice rather than a reward. Detach your feelings from your judgments about how the world should work: your status, achievements, praise and criticism. Also detach from your desire for possessions, your appearance, and your jobs or roles. Have these things or don't have them—and be happy—just because you want to be. Simply sung by Bobby McFerrin: "Don't Worry. BE HAPPY!"

CHAPTER 8

THE POWER OF THANKSGIVING— NOT JUST AN EXCUSE FOR THINNING OUT THE TURKEY POPULATION

SUPERPOWER:
Use the power of Gratitude to train your mind to know what you want, who you are and where you're guiding your life.

"You cannot exercise much power without gratitude because it is gratitude that keeps you connected to power."
— *Wallace Wattles*

The recession, which began in 2007, was long and hard. The number of families forced out of their homes by foreclosure or short sale was appalling—and very sad. Many of the people with whom I worked at the time lost their homes, their savings, even retirement funds. Rather than working to fund a special vacation, send a child to college or buy a new home, salespeople were working to pay the bills, hoping they would not have to sell their homes, have their car repossessed or cancel their health insurance.

A prolonged period of negativity like this can reinforce and strengthen what psychologists refer to as "negativity bias," a propensity to focus on real as well as perceived problems. "Your brain is simply built with a greater sensitivity to unpleasant news," notes Hara Estroff Marano, writing for *Psychology Today*.

Studies conducted by John Cacioppo, Ph.D., then at Ohio State University and now at the University of Chicago, demonstrate that the brain "reacts more strongly to stimuli it deems negative. There is a greater surge in electrical activity. Thus, our attitudes are more heavily influenced by bad news than good news."

Rick Hanson, neuropsychologist and a member of U.C. Berkeley's Greater Good Science Center's advisory board, describes it in this interview with *The Atlantic:* "The problem is that the brain is very good at building brain structure from negative experiences. We learn immediately from pain—you know, 'once burned, twice shy.' Unfortunately, the brain is relatively poor at turning positive experiences into emotional learning neural structure."

When you don't actively focus on what is right in your life, negative thoughts can triumph—over and over again. So, the challenge I faced was how to help my agents overcome the powerful, pervasive negativity propagated by the recession and return them to a more positive, happy and productive state of mind.

How did we become so attuned to negativity?

It isn't too difficult to imagine why focusing on negativity evolved into such a powerful habit. During most of our history, humans did not have the advanced technology, secure shelter or weaponry we have today. The world was far more threatening when we lived in caves or just slept under the stars. We may be at the top of the food chain now, but take away our armor, fences, guns and secure living structures, plus all the technology we've created in the past few hundred years, and we'd move way up the list of potentially endangered species.

Unlike today, our ancestors faced every day knowing there was a strong possibility they'd be eaten by some big, hungrier predator, like cave bears, cave lions, other primates, saber-toothed cats, or perhaps even those pesky, predatory giant chipmunks! Survival required ancient *Homo sapiens* to focus on danger before danger focused on them. Over millennia, our brains became hypersensitive to signs of danger so that we could act, hopefully before being eaten. And, even though today there is very little chance you'll be skewered by giant eagle talons as you leave home in the morning, as a species, we have not yet evolved beyond our negative focus.

Like all habits, negativity bias begins with thoughts: "Watch out for lions, tigers and bears—or get eaten."

How these thoughts became so habitual is explained in verse by Mahatma Gandhi:
- Keep your thoughts positive, because your thoughts become your words.
- Keep your words positive, because your words become your behavior.
- Keep your behavior positive, because your

- behavior becomes your habits.
- Keep your habits positive, because your habits become your values.
- Keep your values positive, because your values become your destiny.

Your words, behaviors, habits, values and ultimately your destiny all begin with thoughts. It makes sense, then, that to change a behavior or pattern, you must change your thinking.

So, the next question is: If you want to overcome negative bias, how much more positive versus negative thinking does it take? There is no one answer to that because there are so many variables when it comes to human psychology. But there is some research that gives us a hint.

John Gottman and Nan Silver, writing for *Psychology Today*, found that sustaining a stable marriage requires at least five times more positive feeling and interaction between husband and wife than negative.

In his book, *The Happiness Trap*, author Russ Harris says that 80 percent of everyone's thoughts contain some negative content. It sounds like we have our work cut out for us. Apparently, it's normal to have negative feelings—it's part of our evolutionary heritage. We're continually scanning our immediate world, looking for problems to solve. But what used to be problems like, "How do I outrun this 600-pound, snarling cave bear?" are now, "How to I outrun the bill collectors?" An email from the IRS is less a physical threat, but no less scary than the cave bear in our subconscious.

It doesn't help that negativity bias is increased by "worry time," which as you know (unless you skipped Chapter 4) has harmful effects on both your attitude and your health. It can shrink brain mass, lower your IQ, and make you prone to heart disease, cancer and premature aging. It can intrude on every interaction we have, harm or even destroy relationships, and make it difficult to function productively.

> **Combating negativity is fundamentally a matter of balancing input.**

The challenge I faced during and in the immediate years following the recession was how to get my salespeople to increase their positive thinking enough to overcome their heightened focus on negativity. All I knew for sure was that it was going to take a potent dose of positive energy to slow down the runaway negativity train we were on.

Through the years, I've discovered several ways to infuse positive thoughts into my brain—self-talk, affirmations, meditation, avoiding negative people and hanging with cool, positive people. Perhaps my favorite and most useful (not to mention easy) method for balancing and overcoming negativity is Gratitude.

Melody Beattie, the author of best-selling self-help books, gives this glowing testimonial for gratefulness:

"Gratitude unlocks the fullness of life. It turns what we have into enough, and more. It turns denial into acceptance, chaos into order, confusion into clarity. It turns problems into gifts, failures into success, the unexpected into perfect timing and mistakes into important events. Gratitude makes sense of our past, brings peace for today and creates a vision for tomorrow."

My favorite, and much shorter, quote of all time comes from Ralph Waldo Emerson:

"We become what we think about all day long."

If you focus on the pile of unpaid bills on the kitchen counter, you will act in ways that perpetuate or increase your financial woes. Spend more time thinking about how prosperous, successful and lucky you are, and you will work in ways that enhance prosperity.

Keep in mind that if researchers are correct that it takes about five times as many positive thoughts to balance the negative, then it's going to take a bucketful of positive to turn around a severe negative spiral.

"There is no better opportunity to receive more than to be thankful for what you already have." — *Jim Rohn*

When you make clear, emphatic statements (to yourself or others) of what you are grateful for, the message to your subconscious is: "Good job, Dude! Let's do that again."

"Gratitude is a vaccine, an antitoxin and an antiseptic."
— *John Henry Jowett*

By focusing on the good around us, we train our minds to search out what's right in our environment and to take the steps necessary to attract better outcomes into our lives. After years of studying and developing a gratitude routine, I've discovered that it is most effective when I use a four-pronged approach. I give thanks for what I enjoy about my life now, as well as to the people who challenge me to grow and learn. I also give thanks in advance for achieving my goals, and for the person I am or am becoming.

Be grateful for those things that you have now—things that you judge as good. This can include any area of your life that you believe is going well—good relationships, success at work, a good workout routine. It can even be as simple as being thankful for a great cup of coffee that morning or a beautiful sunrise: "Thank you for this gorgeous morning."

One way to reinforce the work of the subconscious is through gratitude statements. When you achieve a goal, no matter how small, give thanks to yourself or others who were involved. Give yourself a gift of time off, a special dinner or a purchase of something sweet.

The best way to incorporate this achievement and happiness tool, however, is by showing your gratitude every day. First thing in the morning, make a list of people and things for which you are grateful. This will not only reinforce the achievement process; it will help you begin each day on a positive note. For example, if you continuously message that you are grateful for a strong, healthy body, your subconscious will help you to maintain that state by increasing your energy and desire to work out, decreasing your craving for fatty foods, increasing your taste for healthy, nutritious food, etc. The subconscious is a beautiful partner, adjusting your focus and assisting you in obtaining the things you appreciate.

"Feeling gratitude and not expressing it is like wrapping a present and not giving it." — *William Arthur Ward*

Addressing your feelings of gratitude to your subconscious reinforces your actions, but what about the people who support and love you? It is important to thank them for their contributions to your life—for the maintenance of the relationship and to foster future love and support. Here are some suggestions for demonstrating gratitude:

1. Remind them of what they did for you and the positive effect it had on your life.
2. Do something nice for them: take them to dinner, wash their car, give them a gift certificate to the movies, rebuild their transmission.
3. Reciprocate when possible. Be there when they need love and support.
4. Offer to do something you know they don't enjoy doing, like cleaning their gutters, waxing their car or cutting their toenails (be careful who you offer that one to).
5. Verbalize your feelings. No matter what else you do, take them by the hand and tell them how much you appreciate them.

Be grateful for the people and situations that challenge you the most. You are the sum of all your experiences—the good, the bad and the ugly. Some of the people who have challenged you the most have also helped mold you into the person you are today. You may not be a big fan of your ex-boss or ex-spouse(s), but consider how you grew and strengthened as a direct consequence of a relationship you found so problematic at the time. Thank them for their contribution to your growth.

Challenges build strength and character. People don't learn and grow by surrounding themselves with yes-men who tell them only what they want to hear. People thrive when they are stimulated to question their beliefs in the face of differing opinions. Yes, you may want to smack them at the time (not). Later, after you apologize for the black eye, let them know how much you appreciate their honesty. Here are a few more ideas of how to show appreciation for those "special-grrrr" people in your life:

1. When they are speaking to you, shut off your listening filters, paper-clip your lips together, sit on your hands and listen intently. Even if you don't agree, there is no reason to argue. Remember that their opinion is as likely to be right as yours. If you think they're wrong, resist the urge to tell them so. When they finish, ask any questions that may help clarify their position. Thank them for their opinion.
2. If they push you to take a risk and do something that you would typically resist, thank them and, if appropriate, let them know how helpful their advice was.
3. Comment on social media about what a help they were and how much you appreciated it.
4. Offer to challenge them when it feels appropriate—always with love and compassion.
5. Let them know how much you appreciate the manner in which they delivered their feedback. If you don't like how they communicate when challenging you, plant drugs in their car and call the police—NO, don't do that! Just lovingly let them know how you would like them to communicate with you in the future.

This can be a tough one. Several times each year, agents come to my office in tears because a client has been verbally abusing them. Some men take the opportunity to insult and dominate women who they believe are likely to take their crap because they want or need the business. My advice is always to sit down and calmly tell the client that it is not okay for them to yell or demean you (or whatever they've been doing). Let them know precisely how you expect to be treated in the future and assure them that if they commit to that, you'll be happy to continue serving them. Otherwise, they will need to hit the road—Jack!

Be Grateful for Goals You Are Going to Achieve. One way of demonstrating gratitude for what you plan to achieve is by setting specific, detailed goals. Embedding goals deeply into your subconscious is like programming a GPS in your car. It not only shows you the way to your destination, but a voice (in your head) also alerts you when you make a wrong turn and instructs you how to get back on the right path: "Turn right, or you will suffer a severe financial setback," or something like that.

When you reach a goal, what then? Maxwell Maltz, the author of *Psycho-Cybernetics,* wrote that the primary function of the subconscious servo-mechanism (aka the Reticular Activating System or RAS) is to give you what you want or, more accurately, what you expect. The process of consciously selecting and incorporating goals into your belief system tells your subconscious what you expect out of life. When it delivers, when you achieve a goal, it looks for validation—gratitude. If you feel disappointment, let down, or simply move onto the next goal, your subconscious can become confused about whether assisting with the fulfillment of goals is the right thing to do. This mixed messaging can diminish the effectiveness of future goals. The subconscious is a great tool but, like computers, it is very literal, requiring specific, clear instructions.

Gratitude statements can also work like affirmations. Stating gratitude for what you are creating—your goals— makes it clear to your subconscious what you have chosen to accomplish. Always word your statements as if they have already manifested. If you speak of them as being in the future, they will remain in the future.

A statement like, "I am going to quit smoking," asks your subconscious to support you in a never-ending, futile quest to quit smoking. Instead, try this: "I am a healthy and happy nonsmoker," or "I am so happy to be tobacco free." Hear the difference? These statements suggest to your subconscious that you no longer smoke. It will then open your perception to a worldview where you are a nonsmoker. You may begin spending more time with nonsmokers and less with smokers. You may lose some of your cravings for nicotine or be attracted to someone with an excellent plan or product to help you stop smoking.

If you are working a plan to double your income next year, write, "I am so grateful that I worked my plan and am enjoying an income that is twice what I made in my previous year."

Fake it 'til you make it.

There are always those who have difficulty with "fake it 'til you make it." They feel that it is dishonest, hypocritical. Give me a break!! Take the stick out of your, you know, ear. Yes, faking it requires that you accept something as true that has not yet happened. You get to pretend, dream, fantasize. You did it all the time as a child; you need to get your chops back. In Chapter 1, I mentioned Dr. Judd Baslotto's experiment with free throws. The group that only practiced mental free throws without going into the gym were "faking it."

Resisting effective practices like "acting as if" or "fake it 'til you make it" is an excellent way of avoiding self-responsibility, denying that you have the power to change—change being scary and all, not to mention difficult. So, what's wrong with scary or difficult? You have something better to do than improving your current life, achieving the life of your dreams? Give it a try. You might also read Wayne Dyer's book, *You'll See it When You Believe it*—an obvious play on the phrase, "You'll believe it when you see it." Dyer's version follows the formula that you will see, or manifest, something when you believe that you will; that if your belief is intense and focused, you will act in ways to make it real.

Be Grateful for who you are or who you are becoming. If you are working to change a behavior or habit, or want to reinforce your most cherished values, thankfulness can help. If you recognize behaviors/habits that you want to change, or that you believe need to be adjusted to achieve your goals, create gratitude statements that reinforce your new behaviors or habits.

If you already use affirmations to affirm your goals, reword them as gratitude statements and add them to your daily gratitude time.

I am thankful for my strong, healthy body.
I am so grateful to be in love with the person of my dreams.
I am thankful for my loving, responsible children (remember, fake it 'til . . .)
I am grateful that my income doubled in 2017.
I am thankful for my trip around the world in 2018.
I am thankful that I meditate every day.
I am grateful that I tell at least three people each day that I love them.

Reinforce your values: "I am so grateful that I am an honest and trustworthy person." "I am grateful for remaining calm when those around me are upset."

Treat yourself regularly to something you enjoy, a midweek movie, a special dinner, a Rob Zombie marathon.

Accept compliments with a simple "thanks." Fight the urge to diminish your role with responses like "Thanks, but it was a group effort," or "Thanks, but you would have done the same."

Positive self-talk. Look at your reflection in your bathroom mirror and give yourself a compliment: "Hey, you look good. All the good eating and exercise has worked."

If you use a gratitude journal, add positive statements about yourself to the list you write each morning: "You are gorgeous. Yes, I'm talking to you, ya gorgeous specimen."

If you are feeling guilty for not following through on a promise, blaming yourself for something or just being self-critical, stop, clear your mind and forgive yourself.

The Many Benefits of Giving Thanks

Samantha Smithstein, Psy.D., wrote in *Psychology Today*: "There are increasing indications that feeling grateful can have a powerfully positive effect on our lives, health, psychological and emotional well-being. Kids who experience more gratitude do better in school, set higher goals for themselves, derive more satisfaction from life, friends, family and school, and are less materialistic and have more desire to give back."

Research by Jeffrey J. Froh, an assistant professor of psychology at Hofstra University in Hempstead, N.Y., has found that adults who focus on what they are thankful for are more optimistic; report less depression and fewer physical complaints; and sleep better.

I could list many more studies to prove to you why thankfulness is so essential. But paper is getting more expensive as our forests are clear-cut. So, if you aren't yet convinced, whip out your favorite smart gadget and Google it!

Daily Gratitude writing can be challenging—I know. Here are some tricks of the trade to keep your efforts consistent:

1. It starts with a Gratitude Journal. You can use anything, of course—an old half-empty notebook works fine, but it motivates me to use a gratitude journal, which you can purchase at any bookstore, many gift stores or even drugstores. It's good to see that thankfulness is catching on. But even with a fancy, leather-bound, expensive book of blank pages, I was still having a problem with consistency.
2. It helped me to find accountability partners. I began each day emailing or texting three gratitude statements to my daughters and their significant others. The side benefit was that they would email me back with three things they were grateful for that morning. If you live any distance from your grown children, sharing what you are all grateful for each day helps to keep you close as a family. Of course, your accountability partner could be a friend or colleague. Be sure to choose someone who is not overly judgmental and who will share their gratitude statements.
3. Pay a gratitude visit or write a letter to someone who has helped you in the past.
4. As you go through your day, notice when some-

thing occurs for which you are grateful. Write or say out loud how grateful you are. If another person is involved, tell them immediately how much you appreciate their contribution to your life.
5. While reinforcing the positive, remember to notice when your mind is drifting into negative thinking. Then stop! Silva Mind Control used to teach people to use a trigger phrase like "Cancel, cancel," prompting the mind to release the negative thought. Then take a moment to focus on the positive. Give thanks.

SUPERPOWER SUMMARY

> The SuperPower you are invited to liberate here is the power of gratitude. Using the power of thankfulness, train your mind to know what you want, who you are and where your life is headed. Be grateful when things go your way and when they don't. Embrace the reality of our chaotically perfect world and be thankful each morning that you have another opportunity to enjoy the ride.

CHAPTER 9

THE POWER OF CREATIVITY

SUPERPOWER:
The ability, willingness and courage to access your natural creativity.

"Don't think. Thinking is the enemy of creativity. It's self-conscious, and anything self-conscious is lousy. You can't try to do things. You simply must do things." – *Ray Bradbury*

Creative people—inventors, writers, scientists, painters—will often say that their best insights appear when they are not thinking. Creative ideas seem to pop into their heads while on a bike ride, mowing the lawn, sleeping or awakening. This is because the most prolific source of creativity resides in the subconscious. The question for those seeking creative ideas is, "How do I access this subconscious goldmine?" It can seem so close yet so far away.

Even before all the research into brain waves, people seeking creativity would often keep notebooks and pens beside their beds to record creative thoughts, which often rose to the surface as they were waking. They didn't know why this was so effective, but it was and still is.

In 1924, a German physiologist and psychiatrist named Hans Berger invented the electroencephalogram and began the study of brain waves. His and subsequent research has shown that, as you go through the wake-up progression, your brainwave frequency speeds up. When you are asleep, your brain is in delta, the lowest frequency. As you begin to awaken, your brain activity increases to theta. In theta, you start to access creative ideas from the subconscious. Theta is the state you may enter when engaged in repetitive activities like driving, mowing, walking through a forest, chopping wood, carrying water.

Next, before awakening in beta, you pass through alpha. Alpha waves are present when you are in wakeful relaxation with eyes closed, like while daydreaming or engaged in some form of meditation. When they are present, alpha waves quiet your mind, clearing it of distracting thoughts. With the use of biofeedback, alpha waves have been shown to reduce anxiety and depression.

So, as you begin to awaken in the morning, the frequency of your brainwaves speeds up, passing through theta, then alpha on the way to beta. As you move through theta and alpha, you are in the gateway of the subconscious. In theta, you connect with your most profound creativity and inspiration. The border between theta and alpha is the best range for creative visualization, where you can create your reality by programming your subconscious. Alpha is also the voice of your intuition. It is a state where you experience heightened concentration, learning, memory and imagination.

"One should never impose one's views on a problem; one should rather study it, and in time a solution will reveal itself."
—*Albert Einstein*

Self-Meditate

Kind of like self-medicate but without, you know, drugs. I realize that some people have resistance to meditation, thinking it is a New Age, hippie-type catnap. But, like it or not, you meditate all the time. You just may not be aware of it.

Physical Meditation: When you are mowing the lawn, and notice that the constant brain chatter has stopped, you are meditating. When you go for a walk or sit on a beach and observe the lack of inner dialog, you are meditating. You can turn any repetitive activity into a mindfulness meditation. Instead of rushing through the action as you might typically do, pay careful attention to every detail.

In the half-hour it takes to mow the lawn, do you spend your time mentally solving problems, worrying about the outcome of actions recently made, or merely rushing so that you can get to the next chore? Instead, turn mowing into a new experience by being present. Take slow, deliberate steps; notice that, when you walk, some muscles are contracting while others are releasing. Notice the patterns created as you cut the grass. Breathe in the smells; notice the sound patterns in the roar of the motor. Don't analyze what you notice; observe with a quiet mind. Immerse yourself in the activity and later see how you did not spend this time worrying about work, or money, or parenting, or anything. You were present with your surroundings. Present.

Breath Awareness Meditation: Many have difficulty clearing their minds of the internal dialog. To demonstrate, I sometimes have my students close their eyes and see how long they can go without thinking. It's more difficult than it may sound. Most people have a hard time making even 10 seconds before thoughts intrude.

It helps to focus your attention on something. One popular form of mindfulness meditation is breath awareness. Get into a comfortable position, sitting or lying on the floor, or sitting in a chair—it doesn't matter which, as long as you're stable so you don't fall over should you fall asleep. Don't worry about folding your legs in a lotus position or holding your fingers just so. These physical stances are helpful to some, symbolic of the state they are trying to accomplish. For now, sit or lie comfortably and close your eyes—or you can leave your eyes open or work it both ways. Some find it helpful to listen to soft music, but you may prefer silence. There are also guided meditations available online that are very helpful when getting started with meditation.

There are several ways to focus on the breath. You can feel your tummy rise and fall as your diaphragm expands and contracts, or perhaps notice the air moving in and out through your nose or mouth. Don't "think" about the movement of air; don't label or analyze it. Notice the sensation of the air moving against your skin.

It is important to know that you are not trying to accomplish anything. You're not hoping for an epiphany, not trying to become enlightened, not solving any problems. You are simply being. THOUGHTS WILL INTRUDE. This is normal. Don't get anxious when you notice yourself thinking. Don't get angry or feel guilty. Don't smack yourself in the forehead. This is just part of the process. As soon as you notice the thought, take a moment to acknowledge it, then gently see it flowing through your body, out into the universe, and come back to your breathing. That's it.

Notice when you have thoughts, then gently go back to the breath. It isn't about training your mind to have no thoughts. Just don't follow them when they pop up. Briefly notice what thoughts arise, then gently let them go.

Body Awareness Meditation: This is a process I use to take my students into a deep meditative state. There are many ways of focusing attention on the body. Here is an example of what I say to induce students into a peaceful, tranquil space:

Begin by getting comfortable, sitting or lying down, and close your eyes. Take a deep breath in through your nose and, as you exhale out your mouth, feel your body begin to relax. Now feel a warm, relaxing liquid flowing in through the top of your head. As the warm liquid relaxation flows down through your forehead, notice how the muscles in your forehead release and relax as all of the tension you were holding onto just melts away. As the warm, relaxing liquid flows down through your eyes, notice that the muscles around your eyes are becoming soft, releasing, relaxing. As the warm liquid flows down through your jaw muscles, feel the tension you've been holding in your jaw and just let it go. And if your lips part it's okay. Allow your entire face and head to release and relax as the warm liquid flows down through your neck and into your shoulders. Feel the tension melt away as your muscles let go—releasing, relaxing.

This process goes on until you have moved the liquid down through every part of your body. When you get to your legs, notice how when you release your muscles you can feel gravity pulling your legs down into the chair. And finally, after releasing the tiny muscles in your feet and toes, see the liquid relaxation flowing out the bottom of your feet and down into the earth, carrying with it all the stress you were previously experiencing.

This exercise can stand alone as a body awareness meditation or, as I use it, a way of relaxing your body and mind in preparation for a visualization exercise or other form of meditation.

Another form of body awareness is to pick one part of your body and focus on it. If you focus on your right hand, notice the temperature of your skin, the feeling of pressure where your hand meets your leg or the arm of the chair. See if you can feel the blood pulsing through the veins. Perhaps you can feel it flowing through your fingers. Don't think about it, don't analyze or label sensations, just be aware.

There are other methods of meditation to discover. You'll find a lot of information online. Guided meditations are very helpful. Meditation apps are plentiful on the Internet; some good, some not so good. Try a few out and see what works for you. But it can also be quite helpful, when getting started, to join a meditation group.

7 Deadly Creativity Blockers

Due to the ever-popular "fear of failure" and its kissing cousin, "fear of success," countless great creative ideas never make it into conscious awareness. The following are some common ways in which we sabotage creative insight:

1. **Narrow thinking:** There is never one answer to any problem. Be open to unexpected solutions, perhaps emanating from unforeseen sources. If you always know the answer, there is no reason to get creative.
2. **Logical thinking:** This can result in negating ideas because they are new or dangerous, or because you don't currently have the tools or knowledge to make them work. If you could only imagine that

which you can now achieve, there wouldn't be much creativity or innovation in the world.

A great example of creating something currently unobtainable lies in President John F. Kennedy's address to Congress on Urgent National Needs on May 25, 1961:
"I believe that this nation should commit itself to achieving the goal, before this decade is out, of landing a man on the moon and returning him safely to the earth. No single space project in this period will be more impressive to mankind, or more important for the long-range exploration of space."

When the President challenged the country to put a person on the moon in less than ten years, we did not have a rocket that could make the journey. We didn't have rocket fuel to power the rocket we didn't have, and didn't have a landing module, space suits, heat shields, or thousands of other components not yet invented and manufactured for the flight to take place. About all we had at that point was orange Tang and a desire to beat the Russians. It was the president's illogical, seemingly impossible vision that resulted in Apollo 11, the first manned mission to land on the Moon—on July 20, 1969.

3. **Following the rules** (my personal favorite): Creativity is a violent act. It is the tearing away of old, arbitrary rules. Pocket calculators killed off slide rules. Smartphones killed off pocket calculators. Electric lights eliminated gas lights. DVDs replaced VHS tapes. Digital is ghosting DVDs and Rap replaced Rock. As an old rocker, I'm still pissed about that one!

Creative rule-breakers have been persecuted throughout

history, even killed to protect the status quo. The Italian astronomer and physicist Galileo Galilei was tried and convicted for publishing his evidence that supported the bizarre theory that the earth revolves around the Sun. The Catholic Church vehemently criticized his findings for going against the established scripture that placed earth and not the sun at the center of the universe. Galileo was found guilty for his heliocentric views and was required to abandon his opinions. The authorities sentenced him to house arrest, where he remained for the rest of his life, and his offending texts were banned.

Similarly, German authorities deprived Albert Einstein of his posts in Berlin and membership in the Prussian Academy of Sciences for espousing his General Theory of Relativity and for his pacifist politics which roused violent animosity from right-wing members of German society. Hitler's goon squads seized his property and burned his books in public. Einstein, living in California at the time, never returned to Germany.

To be creative, you need to be willing to break some rules. Go ahead and try it—it can be fun. Just watch your back.

    4. **Being Practical:** One of the best ways to stifle creativity is to evaluate the practicality of a partially formed idea. Take the editor who told Walt Disney he lacked imagination or the publishers who rejected J.K. Rowling's proposal for a novel about a young wizard—really, take them! Close to my heart, as an old rock and roller, was the Beatles' audition with Decca Studios on January 1, 1962. One of the biggest mistakes in music industry history was Decca rejecting the band, selecting Brian Poole and the Tremeloes instead. I

Googled them. Ever hear of *Three Bells* or *I can dance?* Yeah, me neither. Ever hear of *I want to Hold Your Hand* or *Sergeant Pepper's Lonely Hearts Club Band?* I rest my case.
5. **Taking Life Too Seriously:** Creativity is not pretty or proper or always welcome, and difficult if we are too wrapped up in conformity, consistently maintaining the cherished status quo. If you want your mind to be creative, you must lighten up and let it out to play.
6. **Fear of Being Wrong:** Creativity is the act of bringing something new into the world. If you are not too fearful, not trying to be too careful, you will fail many times before achieving your vision. Abraham Lincoln, elected president in 1860, did not exactly have a smooth path to the White House.

1832	Lost job; defeated in bid for the state legislature
1833	Business he started fails
1835	Personal love (Ann Rutledge) died
1836	Suffered from a nervous breakdown
1838	Defeated in attempt to become Illinois House Speaker
1843	Failed to earn party nomination for Congress
1848	Failed to be renominated for Congress
1854	Defeated in his run for Senate
1856	Failed to be nominated for vice president
1858	Defeated in run for Senate

7. **Self-Doubt:** Rather than face failure, ridicule, and fear of the unknown, many will simply declare that they are not creative—a declaration that will not get you into anyone's Hall of Fame. In case you have ever had this thought, just know that it is a fantasy, false, Bantha Poodoo. Everyone has the "ability" to create. Not all are willing to risk it—that's a choice, just a choice.

SUPERPOWER SUMMARY

> To be successful in most industries, you must stand out. Sheep-like conformists are not generally that valued nor well compensated. Since it is hard to stand out doing the same things everyone else does, you will need to access your creativity. The SuperPower offered in this chapter is the ability, willingness and courage to access your waiting creativity.

CHAPTER 10

THE POWER OF SUPER LISTENING

SUPERPOWER:
Turn off all assumptions and judgments and listen with a beginner's mind.

"In the beginner's mind there are many possibilities, but in the expert's, there are few." – *Zen Mind, Beginner's Mind*, Shunryu Suzuki. Also known as Suzuki Roshi, he founded the Tassajara Zen Mountain Center and the San Francisco Zen Center.

You achieve a beginner's mind by dropping all expectations and preconceived ideas—shutting off autopilot—and seeing things with an open mind and fresh eyes—like a beginner, like a child.

Rick Hanson, Ph.D., offered this parable to describe beginner's mind:

"Once upon a time, a scholar came to visit a saint. After the scholar had been orating and propounding for a while, the saint proposed some tea. She slowly filled the scholar's cup: gradually the tea rose to the very brim and began spilling over onto the table, yet she kept pouring and pouring. The scholar burst out: 'Stop! You can't add anything to something that's already full!' The saint set down the teapot and replied, 'Exactly.'"

We discussed the dangers of "full cup" thinking in previous chapters. It is the process of prejudging what we see in the world so that we "know"—can act without analysis—without even listening or noticing the nuance that exists in everything and everyone. We "fill up" our comfort zone with beliefs that are the product of judgments we have made about the world and how it works. In his discussion about "Beginner's Mind," Jack Kornfield, Buddhist teacher and author, tells a story of Seung Sahn, a Korean Zen master who urged us to value what he called "don't know mind." He would ask his students questions such as: "What is love? What is consciousness? From where did life come? What is going to happen tomorrow?" Each time, the students would answer, "I don't know." "Good," Seung Sahn replied. "Keep this 'don't know mind.' It is an open mind, a clear mind."

Here are some significant benefits of listening with Don't Know or Beginner's Mind:

Learning: You can't learn anything while speaking. One of the most common mistakes humans make when communicating with one another is assuming that they know what the other is saying—but those assumptions are based on their unique experiences. If, on the other hand, we realize that we DO NOT know what the other is saying, we create a vacuum which they will happily fill.

Create the vacuum by asking questions, then listen intently to the answers. Don't interrupt. Don't talk about your own experiences. Don't interpret their words through your perceptual filters.

Build a Bond: When you ask questions and listen intently to the answers, you build a lasting bond. With the dismal state of communication today, feeling heard and understood is a rare experience. When was the last time you had a conversation with someone who made you feel that your opinions and feelings were the most important things in the world to them at that moment? How did it make you feel? Did you want to spend more time with that person? Sure. We all like to think that our opinions count, or that they should at least be listened to and taken seriously. When they are not, we feel discounted, put down, perhaps angry and darn right crappy. When someone is apparently not interested in what you have to say, how much time do you want to spend on them? That's a rhetorical question.

Better relationships: If you are always comparing what others say to what you believe, based on your stored belief system, you will experience frustration and disappointment because they aren't meeting your ideal, your expectations. The person you are speaking with will feel criticized and diminished. If instead you look at others with fresh eyes, open to the fact that they are not you—that they have had an entirely different stream of experiences—it transforms your relationship. You see that they are just navigating down the river of life and encountering as many challenges and hardships as you. Instead of a contest, life becomes a collaboration.

Less anxiety: If you are anxious about an upcoming meeting with someone—instead of worrying about how and whether you will convince them to accept your point of view—open yourself up to being curious about what will happen, let go of your preconceived ideas about the outcome and instead embrace not knowing. Embrace being present and be thankful in the moment for what you're doing and who you're meeting.

> **When we abandon our need to know,
> we are free to listen and learn.**

Effective use of many of your other SuperPowers will require Super-Hearing—to understand what others are saying and to hear what you're saying (self-talk). No, when I say "hearing," I don't mean a heightened ability to perceive sound by detecting vibrations—like hearing conversations through a mountain of solid rock or termites digging a mile away. I mean:

> **Listening with a focused desire to understand—
> suspending judgment and resisting the urge to
> compare what we hear to our personal experiences
> of similar situations.**

Thinking that we know how the world works gives us a sense of security. The problem is that what we "know" is often wrong or incomplete because we base it on the limited information we accumulate from exposure to a very tiny piece of the world. The fact that every person on earth is exposed to a unique stream of experiences makes communication—challenging. Here is an example of how a good listener might conduct a conversation:

1. Decide that you will not assume what the other is saying. Enter the conversation with your filters turned off. You have beginner's mind—open and curious.
2. You listen intently while the other speaks, making eye contact, nodding when appropriate, perhaps even taking notes. Never interrupt. And, for **** sake, turn off your phone. If you forget, and it rings, make a point of not answering and then turn it off.

This demonstrates respect for what the other person has to say.
3. Once they stop talking, ask if there is anything else they'd like to add. Wait for the other person to finish.
4. At this point, your mind may try to fill in the blanks to interpret what has been said. Just say NO to your need to interpret! Instead, ask questions. Allow them to clarify, to explain their motives and meanings. Continue probing with questions until you believe that you understand what they are saying.
5. Repeat back to the other what it is you think they said: If, as in the example below, a buyer tells the agent that they want a house with a pool, the agent could say: "I hear that you'd like a swimming pool. Can you tell me what it is about having a pool that interests you?" Once they tell you why they want a pool, repeat that back. Ask them if you understood correctly and give them time to make any adjustments to your understanding.

When you enter a conversation with a beginner's mind, your desire to discover what someone else is thinking begins with the realization that you don't know. Your cup is empty—just waiting to be filled.

The following model demonstrates the problems "full cup thinking" can create. When we filter another person's words through our belief system, we assume that we know their meaning. In this real estate sales example, the buyer thinks that they would like a place to entertain friends and clients. When they filter this thought through their comfort zone, they find the belief that swimming pools are an impressive outdoor entertainment feature. They communicate to their agent that they would like a home with a pool. The agent happens to be the coach of his daughter's high school swim team. When he hears "pool," he filters the buyer's words through his comfort zone and finds the belief that pools are great for people who like to swim, especially for families with kids on swim teams—like his.

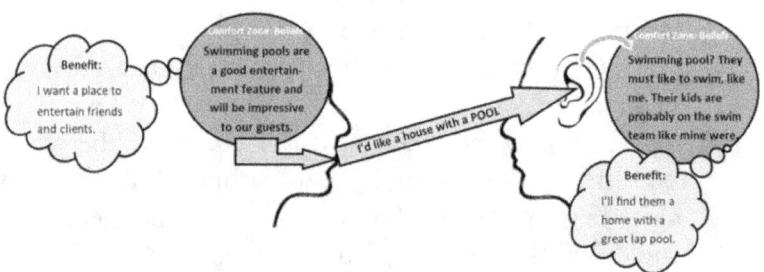

The agent spends the next few weeks showing the buyer homes with good pools for swimming but is unable to find them a home they love enough to purchase. You can imagine the agent's surprise and disappointment when he hears that the buyer bought a home from another agent—especially when he learns that the home has no pool! Instead, there is a large brick patio with an outdoor barbecue, pizza oven, sink and refrigerator—perfect for entertaining friends and clients from the buyer's viewpoint. All that wasted time—for both agent and buyer— could have been avoided with just a few probing questions.

To "hear" the meaning behind the words, do not listen with your ears. Listen with theirs.

The Power of Super Listening

Listen through their perspective, their interpretation of the words they use—based on their experience, not yours. Our unique and elaborate catalog of judgments and labels allows us to view the world with a minimum of confusion and terror. "Knowing" the purpose and function of many common objects allow us to avoid the mind-blowing effects of constant, pioneering analysis. Unfortunately, this ability to form judgments, apply labels, categorize and sort is also at the root of most of the world's problems. In the classic 1967 movie, *Cool Hand Luke*, starring Paul Newman, Luke's jailers called this a "failure to communicate."

Here is a story from a book I wrote and published a few years ago titled *Blood of the Dragon*, which dramatizes this point. It is a lesson taught to the *Last White Knight* by the Wizard Waldrin.

Two kings, Gavin of Galle and Jubah of Carola, were brothers. Their father, King Lordred, had one possession he prized above all others, a golden chalice that was said to have healing powers. Whether the cup indeed possessed such power, I do not know, but Lordred did live a long and robust life. Before his death, Lordred became disgusted by the way his two sons fought incessantly over who would take possession of the chalice after he died. In an attempt to mitigate their bickering, Lordred proclaimed that his sons would share ownership of the prized cup. Each son would house the vessel at his castle for a year, then deliver it to the other son for the next.

After Lordred's death, King Jabah, being the oldest, got the chalice first. There was little love between the two brothers and even less trust. That entire year King Gavin fretted over whether his brother would honor their father's dying wish and hand over the cup at the appointed time. As the day for the transfer approached, Gavin became increasingly convinced that Jabah would never surrender this treasure of treasures. He made plans to attack Jubah's castle at Carola should his suspicions prove valid.

Since neither brother felt safe in the other's castle, they agreed that the transfer would take place in a neutral location somewhere between the two kingdoms. Jabah sent word to Gavin that he would bring the cup to the site of the most celebrated battle of the Palonian war. Gavin knew this field well. It was the site of a great victory for Galle over the warrior Kingdom of Palonia.

On the morning of the transfer, Gavin and a division of guards waited in the field for the ceremonious delivery, but Jabah never arrived. Prepared for this deception, Gavin signaled his army to attack the Castle at Carola, and the war began.

"Why did Jabah fail to keep his promise?" asked the Knight. "Didn't he know that he was inviting war?"

"But he did keep his promise," said Waldrin. "He was on the field at the precise time agreed upon."

"But how can that be?"

"Jabah delivered the chalice to a field that was the site of the greatest battle of the Palonian war. For him, however, this was not the battle in which Galle was victorious over Palonia. As I said, Palonia was a warrior kingdom, always doing battle with one or more of their neighbors. The battle Gavin thought Jubah referred to was one in which the much smaller army of Carola surprised and soundly defeated the Palonians. They fought this battle in the field adjacent to where Gavin's army was waiting, separated from sight by a grassy hill. Either brother could have hurled a rock and hit the other as they waited for the rendezvous, but neither learned how close they had been until blood was shed and it was too late."

"Six years of war because of a mistaken location?" asked the Knight.

"Because of a mistaken communication." Waldrin corrected.

"Gavin heard Jubah through the ears of a Carolan. He interpreted his brother's words from his viewpoint–based on his unique background."

**Knowing stifles curiosity.
Curiosity is the surest path to the truth.**

The primary means of satisfying curiosity is "the question." If Gavin had questioned Jubah as to which war he was referring to when describing their meeting place, he might have prevented a six-year war.

"If you speak, ask a question. Unless what you say benefits the other person, don't say it."
— *Denis Waitley, pioneer in high-performance human achievement*

Asking questions is a beginner's mind in action. When you "don't know," you enter a conversation with curiosity that is only satisfied by questioning the other until they are confident that you understand their meaning.

Now what? Do you just sit there smiling at them?

"Listening is such a simple act. It requires us to be present, and that takes practice, but we don't have to do anything else. We don't have to advise or coach or sound wise. We have to be willing to sit there and listen."
— *Margaret J. Wheatley, American writer and management consultant who studies organizational behavior*

It is a nearly universal belief that when someone shares a problem or concern, they are asking for help, seeking our wisdom, expecting a solution. This is especially true of men (perhaps not all, but exceptions are rare). It seems that we guys are born with the fix-it gene—apparently located on the Y chromosome. There is no problem too small or large that we won't attempt to solve. Our motto: Have answers, will blurt. I know, ladies, that it can be infuriating at times, but have pity, we are just wired that way (not that we can't be rewired— don't tell your mate I said that to you). Rather than listening to understand, we attend so that we can formulate a quick solution, dazzle you with our cleverness and make all your problems disappear. I call this the Prince Charming Syndrome.

I was fortunate to learn this lesson from my second ex-wife, who was kind enough to point out that my witty and insightful opinions and solutions were not always requested or appreciated (not exactly how she put it). At first, this was difficult to understand. Why would she tell me about a problem if she was not seeking my expert assistance? What could benefit her by merely watching and listening? Wouldn't an empty chair serve the same purpose? Come to think of it, she may have even suggested that.

What I discovered after repeated reminders was that being heard is a rare and powerful gift. Through time, the simple act of being listened to released most of the anxiety I felt about problems. Now when this magical gift is received, I can think more clearly, consider my options and, in many instances, solve the problem myself.

We feel nourished, respected, worthy, even loved when another person cares enough to quietly sit as we pour out our doubts and fears; we feel respected when they trust our ability to discover our own solutions.

Aren't they ever looking for a solution from us?

Most of the time, people only want to be heard. But there are times when they are seeking our advice or perspective. Do not assume—ask. It will help you remember this vital sequence if you memorize this short quote from Stephen Covey:

"Seek First to Understand, then to be Understood."

This is pivotal. So, across the front of your collarbone would be a prominent place for this tattoo.

To *understand*, listen to their problem, ask questions, and allow them time to clarify and explain. If you perform this part correctly, you may be in a position to be *understood*, to discuss your bright ideas for possible solutions to their problem. No matter how prepared you are to assist, they still may not be looking for answers from you.

Don't make the mistake of thinking the other will feel better if you share your own experience: "I know exactly how you feel. The same thing happened to me last year and..." While you are relaying your story, they are thinking, "There he goes again, talking about himself. Doesn't he even hear me?" This is complicated, isn't it? How can we tell if they want to unload their feelings, or if they would like our advice? ASK.

Once the other has thoroughly explained their problem, answered your questions and affirmed that you understand, sit back and observe. If they just wanted to unload, they may appear relieved and move onto another topic. Or, they may want to discuss a solution they have formulated. If this is not the case, if they seem to be looking to you for a response, you might say something like this: "Boy, I hear you and your anger is certainly understandable. I have had some experience in this area. If you'd like, I'd be happy to share that with you." If they want your opinion, they will let you know. But you may be surprised how often your creative genius just isn't necessary. That can be a real relief.

Be careful what you say; you may be listening

How you communicate with others is important. How you talk with yourself is critical.

"You can think of self-talk as the inner voice equivalent of sports announcers commenting on a player's successes or failures on the playing field. Unlike that sports commentary, which athletes never hear while they're competing, you can actually "hear" what your self-talk is saying. When this is upbeat and self-validating, the results can boost your productivity. However, when the voice is critical and harsh, the effect can be emotionally crippling."
— *Susan Krauss Whitbourne, Ph.D., writing for Psychology Today*

Ever wish you could predict the future? Now that would be a handy SuperPower. You will get a pretty good idea of where your mind is headed—and therefore your life—if you listen to the things you say to yourself. Self-talk is a compelling window into the conversation that goes on, constantly, between your subconscious and conscious minds. This conversation can affirm your strengths or it can argue for your weaknesses. Because of the Negative Bias phenomenon discussed in Chapter 8, most of these thoughts will probably be negative.

Let's say you are at lunch with colleagues from work (in the year 2043) and the conversation moves to the 30th installment of *Pirates of the Caribbean*. You hated the movie and say so. You point out that the series was dead after the 5th sequel and that by the 30th, and after a hip and two knee replacements, Jack didn't have to fake his drunken walk, and that pairing him with a 24-year-old love interest smacked of pedophilia. No one at lunch agrees. Most of them think that it was the best since the first installment. Self-talk kicks in:

Well, that was a stupid thing for me to say. I believe what I said, but everyone disagrees, and some even seem angry. If my boss hears of this, she'll think I have a problem getting along with others. There goes my promotion. I really screwed up this time. Why can't I just keep my opinions to myself?

By the time you finish with this internal conversation, you feel worse than Jack looks. You run to the kitchen, pop an antidepressant and chase it with a tall glass of wine.

Change the Dialog

The first step in turning your self-talk positive is *awareness*. Be aware of the conversation going on inside. When the negativity begins to flow—stop it. Silva Mind Control, a self-help and meditation program developed by José Silva in the 1960s, taught that when you hear the negative dialog starting up, you say, "cancel, cancel." This is a triggering mechanism that tells your subconscious to cut the crap. You can then consciously direct the conversation to the positive—with affirmative self-talk like:

I'm glad I spoke up. That movie sucked. If my colleagues all liked it, fine, but I am welcome to my own opinion.

I am glad that I had the guts to voice my opinion. I'm sure that some of them hated it too but were afraid to say so.

Speaking my mind demonstrates that I am an independent thinker, do not fear criticism and have leadership qualities that the company will respect.

Positive self-talk can lift you up, bolster self-confidence and strengthen your self-image. The critical thing to remember is that, even though this is a conversation, both sides are you. You are not just listening to these negative messages; you're sending them. They are the doubts and fears that reside within your comfort zone.

SUPERPOWER SUMMARY

> To truly listen, turn off all assumptions and judgments and listen with a beginner's mind. Instead of inserting your own experience and beliefs into their explanation, ask the person you're speaking with to clarify. Replace all your assumptions with questions.
>
> Never assume that others are seeking your opinion—they may simply want to vent. If your intuition tells you that they are expecting help, ask if that is the case. If they want your opinion they will let you know. Otherwise, zip it!
>
> How you communicate with others is important. How you talk with yourself is critical. How you feel about you—your self-image—is greatly influenced by the words you think and speak. Because most of us have a bias toward negative thinking, it takes awareness and perseverance to consciously turn negative self-talk positive.

CHAPTER 11

THE POWER TO REMAIN CALM IN THE EYE OF THE STORM

SUPERPOWER:
Detach from the emotional chaos surrounding an issue, focus on the actual problem, and access your creativity and problem-solving abilities.

There is a calm in the center of hurricanes—the eye.

The most violent and dangerous winds are those immediately surrounding the eye—as if the most intense, chaotic motion is attracted to this harbor of calm. Within your metaphorical eye—your center—you will find the power to shelter yourself and others from the raging human storm. Creativity and problem-solving abilities are most readily available when you remain detached from the swirling drama. It is hard to see clearly when you are lured out of the eye and into the human storm. It is difficult to be creative when focused on the chaos around you, and nearly impossible to be present.

Staying grounded can be a bit challenging when your 14-year-old daughter tells you that she is getting a tattoo, dying her hair green and wants to sleep with her boyfriend. Or when you take your car in for its regular maintenance and are told that you need new brakes, a new transmission and tires, so what you expected would cost $100 is now up to $5,000. Or your partner sits you down and tells you, in a panic, that he has run your credit cards up over $100,000 and wants you to declare bankruptcy.

But isn't it selfish to lounge in the eye while people in the storm are crying for help? No! When a challenging problem arises, and those around you are freaking out, the last thing they need is for you to join them in their freak-out dance. They need a cool head who can come up with creative solutions. They need your undistracted best. So, how do you remain in the eye of the storm when those around you are wailing and running for shelter?

As with most things, remaining within the eye must start with intention—you must want to maintain your cool even when those around you are in emotional turmoil. Once you decide to become calm and detached from the chaos, consider a change in perspective—some new habits.

Don't mirror the emotional state of others. It is hard enough to remain calm with your own issues and emotions. If you let yourself be drawn into other people's drama, peace will be difficult to achieve—for you and them. Remember, you are not serving anyone by agreeing and joining them in their upset. You can best help them by remaining relaxed and focused on a solution to the actual problem. The following is another story from my book, *Blood of the Dragon*, which illuminates why it is crucial to detach from the emotional state of others:

One spring morning after the winter snowpack had melted,

the White Knight rode aimlessly through the countryside, lulled by the sucking sound of his horse's hooves in the thick black muck.

Where is the Wizard? Had he forgotten his promise to continue the Lessons?

Slowly, it entered his consciousness that the sound had changed. No, it was a new sound, the voice of a man calling for help. Galden reined in his steed and stared across the field next to the road, expecting to see...Something, but there was no one in sight.

There was a farmhouse on the far side of the field, but the voice was too loud to have traveled such a distance. This was strange indeed, a disembodied plea for help coming from a flat, muddy field. Curious, the knight dismounted and walked cautiously in the direction of the increasingly frantic voice.

"Hello," the knight called, "if you be human, tell me where I may find you."

"Down here," came a yell, "at the bottom of the well. Hurry, please."

The knight ran into the soggy field, using his arms to balance as he slipped and slid his way toward the farmhouse. He nearly slid right into the well but saw the opening in time to fall on his backside and glide to a stop within inches of the open pit. Pulling himself up out of the quagmire, he gazed into the hole, which was about four feet in diameter and fifteen feet deep. At the bottom, a young man and a woman—both covered in mud. The woman lay on her back in apparent distress; the man knelt over her, holding her hand.

"Quickly," he yelled, looking up hopefully. "My wife needs help. I think she's broken her leg."

Galden stared into the dimly lit scene at the bottom of the well, anxious to act but uncertain as to how he should proceed.

"Come on," the man yelled frantically. "Are you deaf? She needs help now!"

The words "selfless service" flashed through Galden's mind as he propelled himself over the edge and down into the well. With no footholds, he naturally fell straight to the bottom.

Unfortunately, he landed on the woman's injured leg, twisted his ankle, and splashed mud across the man's startled face. The woman screamed, then fainted. The man wiped the grit from his eyes, then stared at the knight, dumbfounded.

Fighting to maintain control over his growing rage, the man asked, "What do you think you're doing?"

"You said she needed help," was all the knight could think to say.

"Are you an apothecary?" the man asked hopefully.

"No, I am a White Knight."

"A White Knight," repeated the man, "not an apothecary. Tell me, Knight, do we look like we are in need of an intermediary? The only thing we need, if you are unable to tend her wound, which is now considerably worse than it was a few moments ago, is a ladder."

"Ladder?"

"Yes, a ladder, to get out of this bloody hole!" shouted the man. Then he had a hopeful thought. Perhaps this foolish knight was not alone. Perhaps he was intelligent as well as quixotic. Maybe his companions were fetching the ladder while he jumped in to assist with his wife's ascent. No, Galden's tortured expression made it clear that he was as he appeared—a fool.

For several moments, there was dead silence at the bottom of the muddy pit until the man began to sniff the air. "What is that smell?" he asked, more to himself than to his new, unwelcome companion.

Galden sniffed and smelled it too, a sweet, pungent aroma. Both men looked up and caught a glimpse of a dark blue sleeve at the edge of the opening.

"Wizard?" Galden asked uncertainly.

"Wizard?" the man repeated.

Waldrin's white beard tumbled over the edge, as he looked down upon the strange scene. "Rescuing someone, are we, Knight?"

"I…" was all that Galden could manage.

"I was brewing some tea for the lady," continued the Wizard. "It will keep her body from shock and begin the healing in her leg."

"You two know each other?" interrupted the man, then quickly, "Whoever you are, don't—jump— into— the well. Go fetch my ladder from beside the house and—" He abruptly stopped as he saw his ladder being lowered into the hole.

With some effort, they managed to convey the unconscious woman out of the well and back to the farmhouse. Waldrin tended to her wounds, which were not too severe, and joined Galden on the front step.

By jumping out of the eye of the storm into chaos, the knight was unable to assist the couple at the bottom of the well. As fellow travelers on the road of life, we owe assistance to those in distress. What we don't owe them is our emotional state. Nor can we be of much help if we become as emotionally compromised as those we would like to assist.

Examine your expectations. Do you believe that life will or should always match your expectations—that everything should go your way? No? Then why fall, screaming, out of the eye every time a problem arises, prompting thoughts like, "Oh my God, this is horrible," or "I don't believe this is happening to me again." If you hear yourself reciting these or similar less-than-productive responses when problems arise, perhaps you should examine your expectations.

There is an old saying: Plan for the worst; hope for the best. I buy the first part. Preparing for unwanted results expands your knowledge and skill base and prepares you for whatever comes. But, as we've discussed, hoping for the best (that reality will match your perfect vision) can lead to judgment, anger, stress, high blood pressure, heart disease, obesity and diabetes. Instead, be ready to respond to whatever results arrive. When we bypass the surprise, disappointment, denial, anger, anxiety, pulling-out-the-hair reaction, we move more quickly to brainstorm creative solutions to problems.

Embrace your ignorance. We are naturally uncomfortable with not knowing. But the truth is we rarely know what is going to happen next. And when something does happen, we don't have the foresight to see if it is a good thing or bad—although we always think we do. The truth is, what happens is not good or bad, just a bend in a road filled with millions of bends. What we believe is terrible today may, in retrospect, be a welcome turning point a year from now. Like a passing show, this happens, now it's gone, then this happens, now it's gone. Remember, 110 years from now everyone on earth today will be gone—all new people! How important are your day-to-day dramas?

Be flexible with Change. John Lennon sang, "Life is what happens when you're making other plans." Goals are good—I've been teaching goal achievement for many years. However, it's good to remember that our vision of the future will rarely arrive exactly as we picture it. Life is too complex. Your goals get buffeted and altered by other people's conflicting goals, the economy, the weather, etc. I like to think that my goals nudge me in the direction of my dreams, while I strive to be accepting of actual outcomes.

And finally, remember what is important. Imagine you're a real estate agent on your way to your daughter's soccer game when you get a call from someone you've been showing houses to for more than a year. They just drove by a house they like and demand that you come immediately to show it to them. What do you do? Ask yourself: *What is important?* Ten years from now, will I lament not showing the house to a person who will probably never buy anything? Or will I lament not showing up for my daughter?

"Speak when you are angry—and you will make the best speech you'll ever regret." — Laurence J. Peters or Ambrose Bierce, depending on who you believe.

Perhaps the most destructive emotion that exists outside the eye of the storm is anger. Anger is the voice of your comfort zone refusing to let go of its vision of how the world should be.

Because we feel safe and secure when the world mirrors our vision, we tend to locate ourselves where people agree with our viewpoint. Outside of this idyllic location are a myriad of diverse and often conflicting views. We tend to avoid those to maintain a peaceful existence and, of course, to "be right."

What often happens when someone shares an opinion is that our ego jumps in and compares it with our opinion. If the two differ, we judge the other as wrong. We may respond with anger, set them straight, quickly refuting the "false" belief and argue for our viewpoint—after, of course, chanting the "I'm right" mantra: B*** S***, B*** S***, B*** S*** (sung to the tune of *Bah Bah Black Sheep*)!! Simple, yet effective—sometimes. Sometimes, not so much. If they defend their position, our anger may grow to the extent that we disparage the other person, or even escalate into violence.

What to do? When you become aware of this process, stop and search for some truth in the other person's analysis. Remember, you based your judgment on your unique and limited experience. The other person's experience may be more cogent to this situation—their opinion may be more appropriate, more correct than yours. Really? Yes, really. At least be open to the possibility. Remind yourself that encountering diverse opinions is a learning experience—the only way to grow. Rather than making them wrong, you can say:

"That's interesting, let me think about that," or

"I hadn't thought of it that way. Thanks for the insight," or

"We may have to disagree on this one, but I appreciate you sharing your viewpoint."

Or, if their opinion is too radically different from yours, you can change the subject or realize that you are late for your wedding and must scoot.

Remember that you do not have to defend your ego. Challenging a belief you have personally accepted is not the same as a personal attack. And even if they do disparage you—so what? Does anyone's opinion, even if they are right, change who you are inside, or are they just revealing who *they* are by contrasting their beliefs with yours? In the end, you can retain your opinion without the need to convert to another. Or, you can use the experience to learn and perhaps revise or replace your opinion.

Within the eye of the storm, we are more interested in understanding others and less in having them understand and agree with us.

But what if someone is angry with me—what then?

"The opposite of anger is not calmness; it is empathy."
— Mehmet Oz

We owe it to our clients, family and friends to remain relaxed, alert and focused when challenging circumstances arise. Then we can access our creativity, communication skills and the knowledge we need to help them solve their problems—if they ask us to do so.

For many years I was in a perfect position to deal with angry people—like it or not. As the manager of real estate agents, I was the one who got to meet with the most difficult, angry clients. It would usually begin with an agent walking into my office saying, "I am at the end of my rope. My clients are crazy, angry and blaming me for everything. I told them that they needed to meet with you. They'll be here in five minutes." Oh goody, I get to meet with angry strangers in 5 minutes. At first, I would feel a twinge of anxiety—I mean, who wants to have strangers scream and shout about how crappy your company and agents are? But then I would remember how much I enjoyed these meetings—no kidding. After you get the hang of it, dealing with anger can be fun.

The impetus for these meetings was almost always the same. The clients got angry with the agent for something they believe they did or did not do. The agent, forgetting their communication skills classes, gets his ego bruised and, instead of addressing the issue, responds to what he mistakenly perceives was a personal attack. He defends his honor by denying the clients' opinions and listing all of his previous achievements—that's embarrassing.

So, with the agent/client relationship in shambles, I, Grand Poobah of the office, must clean up the mess and save my agent's commission. No pressure.

Here is what I've learned about dealing with angry people:

First, prepare yourself. If you know that in a few minutes you will be confronted by angry people, sit quietly and tell yourself (self-talk) that these are people with a problem, people in pain. They want to be heard, and, so far, that hasn't happened. You can also repeat some helpful affirmations like,

"I remain calm and empathetic when confronted with anger."

"Anger is just an opinion that has not been allowed to breathe."

"Everyone deserves my respect."

"Everyone deserves the best I can offer of myself."

Don't shy away from the situation. Knowing that angry people will probably be expecting a defensive, suspicious, anxious greeting, surprise them by meeting them at the door with a smile and an outstretched hand. Imagine them as old friends you haven't seen in a while, offer them a beverage, ham sandwich, or whatever seems appropriate, and escort them to a comfortable place to speak.

Thank them for coming in to see you and ask how you can help.

LISTEN! As we discussed in the "Super Hearing" chapter, attentive listening is a powerful skill. As they tell you their story, maintain eye contact; take notes if appropriate, nod your head in understanding from time to time, but never interrupt. If you forgot to turn off your cell phone, and it rings, turn it off immediately.

When they finish, ask if there is anything else they'd like to add. Ask questions if you need them to clarify. Demonstrate your empathy. I would say something like, "I understand why you're angry. I would be angry too."

Address the issue, not the emotion. Do not defend your actions or honor or, in my case, the agent's actions. What is relevant (besides the fact that the angry party feels heard) is the unresolved issue: "You were one of eight offers, and you don't believe that your offer was even presented to the seller. Is that correct?" "Right." "Would it be alright if I ask the other broker to confirm with their agent that they did present your offer? I could also ask that they provide you with written confirmation from the seller that they reviewed your offer before accepting another." Not a bad solution.

But here is the bottom line. The anger is almost always diminished by the time you sit down. When the offended party is expecting you to be defensive or to respond with anger, and you treat them with the respect and attention they deserve, their rage melts like butter on a hot tin roof—or something like that. If not, the fact that you sit quietly and attentively, listening to all they have to say, will almost always smooth the waters. Remember, their anger is more about not being heard and less about the root issue. They are pissed, and no one has been willing to listen to their side of the story.

This same process will work as well in just about any confrontation. Say a neighbor knocks at your door screaming about the fact that your "f***ing dog" just pooped on their begonias for the 10th time. Invite him in, while telling him how sorry you are. Do not defend your dog's honor. Don't demean his cat, which has been using your daughter's sandbox as a litter box. Go through the listening dialog, then address the issue. Let him know that you want to resolve the situation. You might ask him if he has any solutions in mind. If he suggests mounting your dog's head above his fireplace, just laugh and offer to brainstorm a less lethal solution. Perhaps offer to build a fence, keep your dog leashed or in a pen. The experience of being heard goes a long way toward calming the angry person. Powerful, powerful SuperPower.

SUPERPOWER SUMMARY

> The Power to help those in distress (including yourself) is found within the eye of the storm. Remaining detached from the emotional chaos surrounding an issue allows you to focus on the actual problem, and access your creativity and problem-solving abilities.
>
> When confronted with anger, remain calm and objective. Even though it feels like the anger is being directed at you, it is not about you, so there's no need to defend your honor. Listen with curiosity and empathy. Let the angry person know that you understand his viewpoint—even if you don't agree with it. Being heard is a rare and powerful experience. The simple act of listening intently may be all you need do to squelch the anger.

CHAPTER 12

THE POWER TO ATTRACT YOUR TEACHERS

SUPERPOWER:
How to connect with the information you need to achieve your goals.

"If you only do what you know you can, your life will always be as it is today." — *Kung Fu Panda*

Liberating misplaced, inner powers expands who you are, what you can achieve and what you can contribute. The process may require more of you than you are currently accessing, and for that, you may want help. Fortunately, there are teachers everywhere.

I've often told my students that I have no judgment towards people who love their lives just as they are, with no desire to grow or improve. My personal experience, however, tells me that growth is not optional. We all evolve, to one extent or another, as experiences and new information are revealed to us during our day-to-day lives. But if you do choose intentional growth, with the help of teachers, how do you find them?

The Power to Attract Your Teachers

"When the student is ready, the teacher will appear."
— Attributed to The Buddha and others

You are not alone. When you choose a life of intentional growth, there are teachers everywhere to help you in your quest.

Dan Milman, author of *Way of the Peaceful Warrior*, wrote: "Master teachers are found not only on lonely mountaintops or ashrams in the East. Our teachers take the form of friends and adversaries, of clouds, animals, wind, and water."

When we ask, our teachers reveal all we need to know. The question is: Are you paying attention? We call our teachers by our need to learn and grow. Since we are not always conscious of the fact that we're calling, we may miss a message. But don't worry. If they elude you at first, they will be back, and they'll keep coming back until you finally hear. I wrote this display quote for Blood of the Dragon:

> There is nothing more persistent than life's lessons demanding to be learned—subtle at first, gentle waves languishing up the sands of status quo to kiss the tips of indifferent toes, then receding into the infinite ocean of ideas.
>
> Unheeded, lessons will be revealed again and again, with growing intensity: awakening splashes against your ankles, then jolting soaks up to the knees.
>
> One day, as you're walking peacefully along the beach, the lessons you must learn rise up and knock you off your feet with the ferocity of tidal waves.

This is not some mystical mumbo jumbo. Everything you need to live a blissful, loving, peaceful and productive life is all around you. Teachers appear because your senses become attuned to their message. Unlike many self-help teachers, I don't believe that we mystically attract our teachers out of the ether—they are already in our midst. We don't recognize them until the need arises and we outwardly communicate it.

In the 1980s, I desperately desired a way of living more intentionally. Unsatisfied with the randomness of my life, I felt impotent, powerless. One day a friend gave me a copy of Shakti Gawain's book, *Creative Visualization,* which gave me hope that there were ways of creating a life by choice. Telling my friend how excited I was about the book, he informed me that Shakti lived in Mill Valley. I began attending trainings and one-on-one sessions with her. It was working with Shakti that led me to author and spiritual teacher Dan Millman. I loved *Way of the Peaceful Warrior,* so I got in touch with Dan, and we had many private sessions together at his home in San Rafael. It was my need to learn that tuned my perception to the existence of these marvelous teachers.

These teachers are easy to spot because they are literally teachers. But teachers don't have to be people. It can be a situation we put ourselves in so that we can learn.

Patience can be learned in commute traffic or from a demanding child, tenacity from your top competitor, forgiveness from nature. "Forgiveness is the fragrance the violet sheds on the heel that has crushed it," wrote Mark Twain.

I'm not just talking about spiritual growth. If you want to learn how to sing, your senses will become tuned to any source of information that will help you in this quest. You may never have been aware of any voice teachers in your area. But as soon as you decide to become a singer, you run into a voice coach at your daughter's basketball game or read an article about a local teacher. If you had no intention of singing, the voice coach would still be at the game and the article would still be in the paper; you just wouldn't have any reason to notice them.

If growth is not your thing and you choose the status quo, your experiences will tend to reinforce your current beliefs and you will become more and more entrenched in your existing lifestyle. However, have you ever known or heard of someone living a steady, uneventful life who suddenly seems to go crazy—doing nutty, unpredictable things? The stable, reliable husband who, after 20 years of marriage, goes out and buys a red Corvette, starts spiking his hair and listening to rap? If the status quo gets old and a desire for something more arises, new, previously unfamiliar teachers will appear. The point is: Teachers are everywhere and take many forms. You don't need to search the planet for them. When you choose to learn and grow more rapidly, your teachers will appear as if by magic.

How should you go about calling your teachers?

Become more intentional about growth. Focus on the need for guidance, inspiration, ideas, and you open your perception to the lessons you need. A low-volume conversation in the next aisle at a grocery store will bypass your awareness altogether. However, if you are looking for a nanny, and a person in the next checkout aisle is talking about how sad the family is because they can no longer afford their great nanny, your perception is drawn to this conversation.

You direct the focus of your perception by recognizing what it is you want. Write it down. Create a vision board and hang it somewhere where you can see it every day. Focus on where you want to be, and the path will be revealed. To see the path, you must open your awareness—watch for it.

> Expect to receive help—look for it in seemingly unrelated places—and you will find everything you need for your life.

SUPERPOWER SUMMARY

When the student is ready, the teacher will appear. Perhaps a more accurate understanding is: When the student is ready, the teachers who are always around will be seen. Our teachers can be helpful humans, animals, inanimate objects, or a situation we create in order to learn. These ever-present instructors are made known to us by our need to learn. Focus on what you want and your subconscious will arrange for whatever interactions are necessary to gather the information you need to succeed.

One of the trickiest parts of this amazing process is noticing the teachers when they show up. But fear not—if you miss them the first time, they will be back as many times as it takes for the connection to be made. Recognizing teachers can be especially tricky because the teacher and/or his/her message may not be precisely what you expected. Remember, your visions guide you along your path but rarely show up exactly as imagined. Your subconscious may send you on an alternate journey with results as good as or better than what you imagined.

I HOPE THIS WAS FUN
AND
SUPER HELPFUL.

GO FORTH AND PROSPER.
BE HAPPY!
BE SUPER!

SUGGESTED READING

The following are some of the mentors I worked with directly, or I read their books or listened to their recorded programs. I regret that there are too many to list them all. These are some of the standouts. Thank you all.

THE 7 HABITS OF HIGHLY EFFECTIVE PEOPLE
BY STEPHEN R. COVEY

Covey reveals a step-by-step pathway for living with fairness, integrity, honesty and human dignity, principles that give us the security to adapt to change, and the wisdom and power to take advantage of the opportunities that change creates. It is a bit textbook-like but loaded with useful information.

YOU'LL SEE IT WHEN YOU BELIEVE IT
BY WAYNE DYER

I would recommend just about any book written by Wayne Dyer. Wayne began his writing career in the Seventies with *Your Erroneous Zones* and *Pulling Your Own Strings*, sounding like a type-A psychologist. As time went on, he explored spirituality, became a devoted meditator, and inspired millions with *Manifest Your Destiny*, *Wishes Fulfilled* and many others. I raised my kids with help from *What Do You Really Want for Your Children*.

THE FOUR AGREEMENTS
BY DON MIGUEL RUIZ

The agreements are: Be impeccable with your word. Don't take anything personally. Don't make assumptions. Always do your best.

Suggested Reading

THE SEVEN SPIRITUAL LAWS OF SUCCESS
BY DEEPAK CHOPRA

In *The Seven Spiritual Laws of Success,* Deepak Chopra distills the essence of his teachings into seven simple, yet powerful principles that can easily be applied to create success in all areas of your life. Based on natural laws that govern all of creation, this book shatters the myth that success is the result of hard work, exacting plans or driving ambition.

YOU ARE A BADASS
BY JEN SINCERO

This is a refreshingly entertaining how-to guide filled with hilariously inspiring stories, sage advice, easy exercises and the occasional swear word.

DON'T SWEAT THE SMALL STUFF...
AND IT'S ALL SMALL STUFF
BY RICHARD CARLSON, PH.D.

Learn to put life in perspective by making small daily changes in your life. Dr. Carlson reveals ways to make your actions more peaceful and caring, with the added benefit of making life more calm and stress-free. Dr. Carlson published a series of Don't Sweat the Small Stuff books. I recommend them all.

AS A MAN THINKETH
BY JAMES ALLEN

An oldy but goody, Allen teaches about the mind and how to use it to master your world.

WAY OF THE PEACEFUL WARRIOR
BY DAN MILLMAN

This is based on the story of Dan Millman, Marin resident and world champion athlete, who journeys into realms of romance and magic; light and darkness; body, mind and spirit. Readers join Dan as he learns to live as a peaceful warrior. This international best seller conveys piercing truths and humorous wisdom, speaking directly to the universal quest for happiness.

CREATIVE VISUALIZATION
BY SHAKTI GAWAIN

This is an excellent introduction to visualization, exploring how to use your creative imagination to manifest your dreams.

NO MATTER WHAT!
9 STEPS TO LIVING THE LIFE YOU LOVE
BY LISA NICHOLS

Confront your fears, overcome your feelings of victimhood, reclaim your power and step into your greatness.

Suggested Reading

THE TREASURY OF QUOTES
134 quotes from Jim Rohn, business philosopher and mentor to millions.

THE TREASURY OF QUOTES
150 quotes taken from Brian Tracy's journals, lectures and audio series.

THE SEEDS OF GREATNESS TREASURY
A collection of some of the best, beloved "words to remember" by best-selling author and keynote speaker, Denis Waitley.

ZIG ZIGLAR'S LITTLE BOOK OF BIG QUOTES
Quotes to inspire, encourage and motivate by one of the most sought-after personal development trainers in the world.

www.ingramcontent.com/pod-product-compliance
Lightning Source LLC
Chambersburg PA
CBHW052033070526
44584CB00016B/2022